JUST FOR TEENS

THE DATING BOOK

A GUIDE TO THE SOCIAL SCENE

BY JULIE CAHN

A Wanderer Book Published By Simon & Schuster

Designed by
Rebecca Tachna

Manufactured in the United States of America
10 9 8 7 6 5 4 3 2 1
WANDERER and colophon are trademarks of Simon & Schuster

Library of Congress Cataloging in Publication Data

Cahn, Julie.
  The dating book.

  (Just for teens)
  Bibliography:
  Includes index.
  Summary: A guide designed to help teenagers answer questions about dating, romantic relationships, sexuality, friendship, parties, and etiquette.
  1. Dating (Social customs)—Juvenile literature. [1. Dating (Social customs) 2. Friendship. 3. Interpersonal relations] I. Title. II. Series.
HQ801.C26 1983
646.7'7'024055   82-23911
ISBN 0-671-46277-6

CONTENTS

INTRODUCTION

Being a teenager isn't easy. In fact, some people say it's the hardest and most confusing time in a person's life. It's a time when the simple ideas you once had about things, don't seem to work anymore. It's a time when your social world begins to grow very quickly but your knowledge of how to deal with it seems limited.

And, because you're beginning to look like an adult, it's also a time when people may begin to expect you to act like one—and since you've never been an adult before, it's hard to know just exactly what that means.

You are growing, and because of this, so are the demands that are made on you. Chances are you now have more responsibility at home than you did a few years ago, and surely a lot more assignments and tests at school. Even with your friends, it seems there's much more at stake now than there was in your relationships when you were younger.

Sometimes all of these changes can be overwhelming. Other times they can be exciting. So many things are happening to you for the first time that handling any of these new situations well is itself an accomplishment— something for you to be proud of.

Some people say life gets easier as a person grows older, that just living through certain experiences makes someone better prepared to handle them when they happen again. Other people say that life gets harder, that the older someone gets, the more complicated life becomes. Maybe both ideas are true. You'll have to wait until you're older to decide that. All that's for certain now is that you're changing and growing, and that someday soon you'll find that you're not a teenager anymore. But for now, being a teenager is all you can be. Perhaps this book can help to make these years a little bit easier, a little less confusing, and maybe even a little bit more fun.

GOING OUT

Some people call it dating. Some people call it going out. Either way, it means the same thing. Being out alone with a boy, whether at a movie, on a long walk, or sharing lunch together, is different than being out with your parents or girlfriends. It means that at least one of you is interested in the other, or that maybe a third party thinks you could like each other. It's possible that you're just friends, two people who simply enjoy each other's company. Going out alone can give you the opportunity to become more than that, or to simply improve the quality of the friendship.

Basically, when a boy and girl date, it's a chance for them to get to know each other, and a way to find out if they'd like to know each other better.

How Can I Be Sure How I Feel?

Unfortunately, when it comes to figuring out how you feel about another person, you're the only one who can decide. When you're confused, it's a very hard decision indeed. It's not that it always has to be so hard. With some people you may find yourself very sure and clear about your feelings.

But sometimes it's not so easy to know. You may not especially like the way one boy treats you in public, or you may have very strong feelings of attraction for another who may do things that you don't think are right. Maybe you're interested in a boy whom your best friend hates, and since she's someone whose judgment you've always trusted before, how can you trust your feelings? Or what if you're interested in a boy who you know has been dishonest and hurtful to other girls in your class. How could you like him then?

There are a lot of factors that come into play when anybody decides how involved they want to get with another person. Usually we go by our initial reactions, and when we're first attracted to someone, our reactions can be pretty strong. But it's not long before other concerns creep in and we begin to ask ourselves a lot of questions: Is he good for me? Would he be nice to me? Can I trust him? Do I really want to be alone with him?

At a moment when you're in conflict, making the right decision can seem like a very serious matter. But sometimes, if you stand back and get some perspective on the whole thing, you can begin to appreciate that the decision needn't feel so urgent.

Would it help to talk about it with other people? Talking to a good friend can often help. He or she doesn't have the same emotional investment in the decision unless, of course, the person in question is someone she likes also. In that case, pick another friend to talk to. If your friend's a truly good friend, he or she will try to help you understand how you feel by examining with you the things that seem to hold the most importance for you. Maybe your friend will talk about what she's observed about you in relationship to this special person. A friend who knows you well can usually tell without much explanation basically what you're feeling.

But mostly, because your friend isn't caught up in your particular struggle over this other person, he or she can sometimes help you get your feelings under control.

Should I Accept A Date From Someone I'm Unsure Of?

It may feel very serious, but the decision of whether or not to go out with someone doesn't actually have to be such a serious matter at all. Agreeing to go out doesn't have to mean any more than just doing that. Of course, by saying yes you're indicating to the other person that you think you would enjoy his company. But by going out, you are not necessarily saying that you'll go out with him again, or that you'll get physical with him, or that you're game to do whatever he might suggest.

If you're really unsure of the person, you can always arrange a short visit with him. You can agree to meet during your lunch period. Nothing so terrible could happen in an hour. Or you could invite a boy whom you're not sure of over to your house. There, you and your parents make the decisions. If you're feeling uneasy about him there, you can always ask him to leave. Public places are also good with people you're unsure of. There's lots to look at and react to in public, and other people can distract you, if need be, from each other. And, if you're actually concerned for your safety, having other people around can make you feel more secure.

What Do I Do If I'm Afraid?

Generally, it's not a good idea to make yourself too dependent on a person you're not sure you can depend on. If you're worried about how you're going to get home, make sure you know how to do it by yourself. When the boy in question either doesn't drive very well or has the habit of getting pretty drunk or high when he goes out, make sure not to go anywhere that calls for a car. If you're afraid that being alone with this person might mean him pressuring you into a situation you may feel uncomfortable with, suggest a place where you know there will be other people around.

Try to remember that if someone's interested in you enough to want to go out with you, he should also want to take your feelings into consideration. And, if he can't, that is another quality to think about when figuring out your feelings for him.

It's Hard To Trust My Feelings.

One nice thing about feelings is that, despite all the expectations coming from the outside, feelings are something that are yours alone. If you don't like a boy, that's your prerogative—no matter how wonderful your mother may think he is.

Your feelings when you're around the person will tell you a lot. Do you feel comfortable? Do you feel he's listening to you when you talk, and picking up on the qualities that are unique to you? Do you feel you can be yourself around him? When the answer to those questions is yes, you know it.

If, on the other hand, the answer is no, then you have very legitimate reasons to consider whether or not you want to see the person again. People may try and influence you, and it's hard not to worry about what they think. But only you know what you feel.

Trust your instincts. They have important things to tell you about yourself.

How Do I Show A Boy That I Really Like Him Without Scaring Him Away?

There are many ways you can show a boy you like him. Some ways may work and some ways may not, depending on who the person is. It might scare someone off if you were to tell him outright that you had a very serious crush on him. If his feelings for you are wavering, knowing that you're "very serious" could be a little bit much to handle. On the other hand, if he's also got a very serious crush on you, he might be relieved and very happy.

With someone you don't know very well, or at least don't have an intimate relationship with yet, it's sometimes safest not to make too many declarations in the very beginning. There are other ways to show someone you like him, without coming right out and saying it.

Everyone likes to be noticed and recognized for what makes him or her special. If you genuinely are intrigued with someone, you probably have noticed a lot about him already. You probably are aware of how the person likes to dress, what his best subject in school is, the kind of people he likes to spend time with, what his hobbies are, and maybe even some of his favorite foods or songs on the radio. Very possibly, you share a lot of his likes and dislikes; that could be one reason why you find him attractive.

Talking to someone about something that obviously interests him is one way of getting to know him better and showing him that you care about the things he likes and the way he thinks. If you pick the areas that you are intrigued with too, it will show him that you have something in common. If you like the same music, for instance, and you convey that to him, it means that you can probably enjoy going to record stores and concerts together, or simply sitting around and listening to your favorite songs. By doing things together, and sharing experiences, you may find you're growing closer to one another.

And if you feel relaxed and good with each other, that in itself says alot.

But sometimes showing someone you like him involves going a little bit farther out on a limb than simply feeling good around him and talking about areas and interests that you share in common.

Can I Ask Him Out On A Date?

You could always ask him out. Granted, because it's still considered unusual in some circles for a girl to be so assertive, the two of you might feel embarrassed. It really can depend though on how you handle the invitation.

If you know a boy well enough to be interested in him, you probably already know how he might react to being asked out. If he shies away from people who are direct, you could still ask him out, but you may want to play down the point that it's a date.

There are ways of making an invitation sound casual, ways that can take at least some of the pressure off people who might have a hard time handling it. You could invite a boy to join you and a group of friends in an activity. Maybe a friend of yours is also interested in a boy she's too shy to see alone. You could set up a double date for the movies. If you're at the library after school with a boy you'd like to get to know better, you could invite him to have dinner with you afterward, either at home with your parents or somewhere out around town. If your parents aren't home, you could say something on the order of: "My parents aren't home so I was planning on getting a sandwich in town for dinner. Would you like to join me?" Saying it that way sounds friendly and not too forward.

With other boys you might not have to be so careful. Some boys might not be at all threatened or uncomfortable with the idea of a girl asking them out. Boys like this tend to be self-assured and approachable. While you still might not want to make it sound too serious, you could easily enough say something like: "I was thinking of seeing such and such movie on Saturday. Do you want to come?"

When you ask a boy out, the worst that could happen—besides the chance that you might both become embarrassed—is that he could say no. That could make you feel hurt and sorry that you ever asked. But depending on how the boy you like says no, there's also the possibility of at least gaining a better understanding of the kind of approach he seems to be most comfortable with.

And there's one very important thing you ought to gain no matter what your results. Once you've asked a boy out, once you've deliberated on how to say it and when to say it, and experienced all the tension surrounding the moment of actually posing the question—after all that, you should have a much greater appreciation of what boys go through when they ask you out. It should make you more impressed with the boys who do it with poise, and more sympathetic to the ones who seem to be having a hard time with it.

When Feelings Aren't Mutual, What Do I Do?

While love can come effortlessly to almost everyone at some point in life, there are other times when it seems like, no matter what you do, nothing could make it happen. Why it works out one time and not another is often hard to explain.

Timing is one factor. Whether or not you meet a boy at the point in his life when he can be receptive to you or to romance in general, has something to do with it. Maybe he's too young or too caught up in his own problems to respond to even the possibility of a relationship. Or maybe he's going through a stage in which he's feeling discouraged or otherwise not in the frame of mind to get involved. Who you're involved with, and who he's involved with, and how available each of you are, contributes to it not working, too. So does the way your respective personalities interact.

Some people just make better matches for each other than others do. It has nothing to do with looks or whether or not one of you is a better or smarter person than the other. What it has to do with is familiarity and the complicated, unconscious process by which people come to feel attracted to one another.

If a boy you like just doesn't like you, if all your efforts to win his attention have failed, if nothing you do seems to make a difference, you may just have to come to accept that it was not meant to be that you should be together. Try not to take it personally, as hard as that may be. Sure, it's *you* he's rejecting, but for *his* personal reasons, which may have little to do with any of your pluses or minuses.

What If I'm Getting Mixed Messages?

If, on the other hand, you're getting mixed messages, if you have the distinct feeling that a boy likes you, but nothing much seems to be happening, there's a bit more you might be able to do about it. A boy who's on one moment and then off the next is a boy who's confused. In all likelihood, he's more mixed up about himself that he is about you. Maybe he's a little bit afraid of getting close to girls, or worried about his inexperience or whether or not, on a closer look, anyone would really like him. Boys have all the same doubts girls do, and wavering is one way they have of showing it. If you sense that a boy you're interested in has doubts, you may want to temper how you act around him. If you're too forward, you can scare away a boy who's unsure of his feelings. But if you retract altogether, you may not get the best results either. It doesn't take much to make a doubtful boy think you don't like him. Feel out what you think is the best way to approach him considering the situation. When he's being aloof, you may not want to put strong demands on his attention. You probably will feel hurt, but chances are it won't help to let him know at the moment that that's how you're feeling. If he has to ignore you in the first place, he probably wouldn't be in the best state of mind to take on your feelings, at least not with the kind of consideration you would hope for.

It's Hard Controlling My Feelings. Do I Have To?

When you're feeling bad, it's often hard to disguise your emotions. But, particularly with someone you may not know that well yet, you may want to try to exert a little more control over your feelings than you do usually. Nobody wants the responsibility for hurting another person. If a boy gets the impression that you're easily hurt, and if he also doesn't have much confidence in his ability to keep from hurting you, he could avoid getting involved with you altogether.

It might not feel like the most natural thing to do, but sometimes when a boy shows doubts, keeping your distance can help. It's one way of saying, "I respect you and your need to figure it out your way." If, after a while, nothing seems to be changing, you might want to suggest a talk. Try to understand his position; it could help you feel a little bit better about yours.

What About When The Situations Are Reversed?

What about when a boy asks you out and, for reasons that you're sure of, you decide you don't want to see him? Maybe you know enough about him already to know you wouldn't feel good around him. Maybe he's involved with someone else and you think it's nervy that he should have asked you in the first place. Maybe there's something about him that repulses you (however irrational that feeling may be). Or maybe he's just a creep and you don't want to have anything to do with him.

Regardless of your reasons, getting into a discussion about why you don't want to see a boy is generally the hardest way out of it. For one thing, if you are lying, the more you talk and try to explain, the more obvious it will become that you are making up a story. And once you start explaining, you only risk getting yourself in deeper.

No matter how unattractive a person seems, you probably won't want to come right out and say, "I'm not going out with you because I don't like you." That would be mean. It may not seem like the most honest thing to do, but making excuses—short and simple ones like, "I'm sorry, I already have a date on Tuesday," or "Thanks, but I'm busy," or "Sorry, I can't"—usually work. Even if a boy pressures you to give specifics, you don't have to. You can always say, "I just can't," or "I'm sorry, but, as I said, I have things to do." The message will usually come through loud and clear; then it's in the boy's hands to decide what to do about it. If you've actually convinced a boy that you're not seeing him because you have other plans, if maybe you were too specific with him, he'll probably ask you out again. Next time be more vague, and he'll probably begin to feel your reluctance. Even then, some boys, either because they really like you a lot or because they just can't face someone turning them down, will persist. The more that happens, the more the situation can become awkward for everyone involved. Some boys may demand an explanation, or will try to talk you into going out with them. They may want reasons, but you don't have to give them.

It's usually safest and kindest to be as non-commital as possible. Some boys may get discouraged sooner than others, but if you're consistently unresponsive, few boys will hang on for long.

Is Flirting Just Fun, Or A Serious Business?

We learn to flirt at a very young age; usually we pick up the technique by watching others. Flirting can be playful, or it can be serious, but usually it's a little bit of both.

Boys flirt and so do girls, and in both, the same sort of mechanism is operating. You meet a person you like, and rather than let on outright that you're interested, you flirt. This gives the person hints of your feelings but still is an elusive enough gesture to allow you to hide and stay "safe." It is, after all, a noncommital way of saying, "I might like you." Flirting can be as intentional as one person trying to figure out if another person is interested in him or her, or as innocent as two people finding each other cute. That kind of flirting can happen on a bus or in an elevator with a stranger. The whole episode may be no more than a few seconds, but it's still flirting.

Flirting can also be a way of initially getting to know someone. It's giving yourself time to decide what you're feeling and giving an invitation to the other person to do the same. Of course, it takes two to flirt. Without the response of another person, flirting is not fun, and most people will give it up when it's not working. But when a person does respond, it's usually from the way he flirts back that you begin to form ideas about him. Say, for example, your way of flirting is by being funny. Maybe when you like someone, or think you like someone, you try joking with him. If the other person doesn't laugh or joke back it tells you that either he doesn't think you're funny or maybe doesn't feel comfortable with the way you're behaving. But if the person does laugh or can even make you laugh, then you know you have similar senses of humor and maybe a basis on which to begin a friendship.

Can Flirting Be Taken The Wrong Way?

The way a person responds to your flirting has as much to do with him as it has to do with you. Some boys like girls who are very forward. Those boys probably wouldn't be as inclined to pursue you if your way of flirting was limited to little glances when you think no one is looking. Other boys might not like it if you're bold; it may not be the style of relating that feels most comfortable to them. It's not hard to tell how a person is taking it.

But while flirting is usually harmless, it can be hurtful, too. Generally, it's not a good idea to flirt with someone who you know has a crush on you but who you also think is someone you could never really like. Flirting in that kind of situation is unfair—unless of course you're allowing for the possibility that you may change your mind about that person.

Some people expect to follow through when they engage in flirting, other people like doing it just for the sake of doing it. It's good to try to be sensitive to the other person's intentions, if for no other reason than to avoid uncomfortable situations.

Flirting with someone who's unavailable or clearly no good for you can also present problems. Conscious or not, flirting is a way of getting closer to someone and a very clear invitation to the other person to get closer to you. Your better judgment might be saying stay away while your behavior is saying the opposite. The person you're flirting with doesn't know what you're thinking, only how you're acting, and it's based on that that he decides how to respond to you.

If Someone Suddenly Starts Flirting With Me, How Do I Handle It?

Let's say someone you've secretly been harboring a crush on or maybe someone you've never even met before *suddenly* begins to flirt with you, catching you off guard. How do you know what to make of it then? How do you know how to act?

If it feels right, you probably won't even wonder. Something will be happening, something unspoken and spontaneous, and it probably won't be until afterwards that you'll even stop to think about it. Other times, it's hard to know. Flirting just by itself doesn't have to be threatening, but if it makes you feel uncomfortable, you don't have to engage in it. Flirting can be as subtle as flashing a quick glance over at someone and then looking away, and as obvious as telling someone you like his appearance.

If someone is talking to you about something that makes you uneasy, say you've got to go. If someone's getting too personal, asking you questions, for example, that you don't feel comfortable answering, there's nothing wrong with saying you don't want to talk about it or changing the subject. And if someone is touching you and you're not sure how it's meant, how it feels to you, or if you simply don't like it, you have every right to say stop it or to walk away. The best way to judge whether or not someone's flirting means a special interest, is first to watch the person in relation to others and then to watch how the flirting develops in relation to you. If a boy flirts a lot, if it seems to be the only way he know how to relate to girls, maybe you ought not to take his flirting with you too seriously. But if his flirting with you begins to evolve into something different, if the more you both do it, the closer you begin to feel, then you'll know the flirting was hinting at something real. If learning more about each other triggers a genuine curiosity and interest in you, you'll see that flirting can sometimes be a helpful thing.

Sometimes Flirting, Even When I Do It, Confuses Me.

A person has to be in the right mood to flirt. Usually that's when you feel good, but with some people it may be just the opposite. Whatever the reason, if someone flirts with you one day and then doesn't the next, it doesn't necessarily mean he has decided he doesn't like you anymore. Maybe he's just not in the mood. Or maybe he's finding himself getting in deeper than he expected, and what started out as just fun is beginning to feel too serious.

Understanding flirting is complicated because people are complicated. Flirting itself is actually very easy and natural and is sometimes just a fun thing to do. There are no tricks to flirting, no right or wrong ways to do it. People develop their own flirting techniques without even trying. If you don't think you know how to flirt, maybe it's just because you haven't been in enough situations in which you feel comfortable enough to do it. It's tempting, but not usually the best idea to copy someone else's style even if they're very good at it. What's right for them may not be right for you. What they can carry off, you might not be able to, and after it all, you might be left feeling foolish and not a bit like yourself. Your personality is all your own, and the way you reveal it should be just as unique.

What Do I Wear When I'm Going Out?

Your choice of what to wear when you're going out will depend a lot on who you're seeing and where you're going.

If you're seeing someone you've known for a long time, for example, you will probably feel more relaxed about what you choose to wear. If it's someone new and you know you're very interested in him, you could want to feel especially pretty when you're with him. If you're seeing someone you don't know, a person whose tastes and styles are unfamiliar to you, you may, on the other hand, feel very confused and find you have trouble deciding what to wear. Similarly, if you know you're going to a play, and have been to the particular theater before, you'll probably have a ·good idea about the kind of clothing that's appropriate to wear there. Clearly if you don't know where you're going, you will probably be less sure.

But no matter what sort of situation you're in, there are certain basic rules you can follow.

Try to rely on your own judgment. Pick an outfit you feel pretty in—something that's comfortable and makes you feel good about yourself. Chances are if you feel good about yourself, you'll look pretty no matter what it is you're wearing.

Avoid wearing anything that's too tight. It will only make you feel uneasy. Besides, if you expect to be eating, the outfit may get even tighter and you'll feel even worse. Also, don't wear a dress that might slip off your shoulders, for instance. It will only distract you, bother you, and will make you have to fuss with your clothes all night, which isn't always the most attractive thing to do.

A hem that threatens to come down, a zipper about to pop, a waistband held together with safety pins, or a button that doesn't stay closed: these are the things to stay away from, if for no other reason than they demand the attention you should be giving to the person you're with. They also make you more nervous, and who wants to be nervous about a zipper breaking when you're nervous enough already about simply talking and relating. So wear something that fits comfortably and that you can depend on.

If you've been invited to a place or function that you're unfamiliar with, there's nothing wrong with asking your date what's protocol. You'd be glad you did rather than find yourself in a situation where everyone's in dresses and you're conspicuously in jeans.

Unless you're confident enough to carry it off, avoid outfits that are too complicated or flashy. While they may call positive attention to you, an unusual outfit can sometimes also offend or embarrass.

In short, if you're unsure about what to wear on a date, it may help to remember to dress simply, comfortably, and appropriately for the occasion. A simple skirt like a jean skirt, a classic pullover, or a pair of pants that fits well are all good standbys. If you keep a set of these clean and pressed in your closet at all times, it will save you at least some of the hysterics. Remember sweaters when it's cold and light clothes when it's warm.

Always be prepared. You never know when you'll be asked out!

What Do I Say?

Sometimes conversation comes naturally between people. What one person says touches off something in the other, and before they know it, hours have passed without either of them once feeling uncomfortable about what to say.

But then there are other times when, for whatever reasons, two people have difficulty making conversation with one another. Either they are both nervous or shy or they are simply not used to being together in a dating situation.

You may be very comfortable with someone within the boundaries of your school or maybe around your block, but put that same person across the table from you in a restaurant and you may suddenly feel that you're with a stranger. You simply can't think of anything to say to him. Seeing someone out of a familiar context can be hard at first, but generally it doesn't take long to get over the uneasiness of being in a new place together. New places become familiar places quickly enough.

If you are uneasy, you can always start by talking about something that you both know about. If you've got friends in common, you can talk about them. If you recently took the same exam in school, there's always something to say about that. Or if you know you've grown up in the same town, you can talk about what that's been like.

If you can't find any common ground, there's always the news or even the weather. Neither has to be as boring as it may sound. It's how you relate them and what you think about these occurrences that make them interesting.

There's nothing wrong with making small talk at the start of a date; it can help to relax you both. You can chat about your surroundings, and remark on the things you observe. Even a menu in a restaurant can be a point from which to start a conversation.

After all, it doesn't really matter what you talk about—except of course to avoid topics that might be embarrassing to you or the boy you are with. (It's probably not a good idea to talk too much about other boyfriends to a boy you're first meeting, or anything else too personal.) What matters is feeling comfortable enough to enjoy yourself. After that, talking should come naturally.

Who Pays When The Check Comes?

Money and who pays the bill is a sensitive subject. The only way it can be completely avoided is for you to pick a place or activity for a date that doesn't cost anything.

Short of that, there are some ways that you might be able to make the situation slightly less awkward.

Always carry money with you, but especially if you're going out with someone you've never been out with before. It's a precaution against being caught in the spot of not having enough money to cover a bill. That could be even more embarrassing than deciding on who's going to pay.

When the bill comes, wait for a few seconds to see how the boy you're with reacts. If he takes the bill and studies it away from your view, it could mean he wants to pay it. If he discusses it with you, either comments on what something costs or invites you to look at it for any other reason, he probably expects you to share the bill or at least pay your portion of it. If he's hesitating and you think it might mean he either wants or needs you to contribute some money, you may want to volunteer by saying something like, "How much is my portion?" or "Should we split it?"

Think before you go out about how you will

handle this sometimes delicate issue so that, no matter what happens, you won't be caught off guard. There may be some cases in which you feel you'd rather not have a boy pay for you at all. Consider how important this is to you, what your reasons are, and how you're going to convey your choice to the boy you're with. Is it because you know you could never really be serious about the boy and therefore don't want him to be too generous with you? Or is it because it makes you feel uneasy for another, maybe more political reason? Will you insist on paying your way, or if the boy you're with objects, will you let him pay for you? If you can make up your mind before the actual situation comes up, it could ease some of the discomfort at the moment.

If a boy has paid for your dinner or anything else, it's polite to thank him. Even if you didn't enjoy your date, you should say something like, "Thank you for dinner," or "Thanks for the movie." When someone spends money on you it's a kind of gift or way of giving you something. Very simply, it's common courtesy to acknowledge your appreciation.

What Are Some Ideas For Dates?

If you're trying to decide what to do on a date, there's no reason you have to limit yourselves to the traditional movie or dinner out. In fact, sometimes sharing an activity together is easier than sitting face to face or side by side with a person you don't know very well. It can also be a more effective way of learning about the person you're with, and maybe also a chance to have more than the usual fun.

Going for a long walk, maybe through a neighborhood neither of you has explored before, gives you a chance to talk and lots of material for an interesting conversation. If you're walking through a commercial district of a town or a city, there are lots of stops you can make along the way. You can stop for a quick sandwich, ice cream, or anything that looks entertaining such as street performers, pet stores, etc. You can also just window-shop.

Preparing a picnic and taking it on a bus ride, no matter where the bus goes, can be fun. There's nothing to stop you from taking the bus all the way to the end of the line and back again. You can talk, look at your town the way a tourist might, and even pretend you're on a trip somewhere else together. And then there's always the possibility that you might pass something like a fair, bazaar, or garage sale that looks interesting, and you can get off the bus.

Bowling, ice skating, bingo, roller-skating, bike riding, and swimming are all activities that neither of you have to be too good at to enjoy together. Skating can be exhilarating, and biking, especially if you plan a long day trip on the weekend, can be an adventure. Actually, any sport can make you feel good physically and also give you something to talk about afterwards if you should decide to go out to get something to eat together.

If there are a few eating places open around your town at night and you're hungry, you can spread out your courses over a few spots. For example, you can start with an egg roll at your local Chinese restaurant, then go for a hamburger at a luncheonette, and after that maybe go to a bakery for dessert.

Making something or working on a project together can be a nice change from the usual visit to somebody's house. Cooking can be a lot of fun when you're doing it with someone you like. Baking cookies or a cake doesn't take long, and you can decorate them any which way you like. Baking bread is a longer project but it's fun, too, especially the kneading part, and while you're waiting for the bread to rise or bake, there are always other things you can find to do around the house. If you've got all the right equipment and ingredients, making candles can be an easy and quick project. A box of different colored crayons is all you need to make a candle of any color of your choice. Even board and card games can be fun with the right person. You might want to try for variation by making up your own set of rules or adding on a few to make any of the games more complicated and interesting.

What Can I Do If The Date's Not Working Out?

There will be times when you're out with a boy and not having a particularly good time. In fact, you may have had an experience already that was very uncomfortable, tense, or just not what you hoped it would be. When you look back on these experiences they may not seem so bad, but while they're happening they can feel awful.

If you find yourself in a situation that makes you feel uneasy, in danger, or offended, don't feel embarrassed to cut the date short and go home. That goes for being in a car with a boy who's going through red lights or driving uncontrollably. Tell the boy to let you out if you feel worried, and call a friend or member of the family to pick you up. It also goes for times when a boy may be getting more physical with you than you care to be. Ask him to stop. If he doesn't, you may want to end the date right there. A boy who's mean to you or getting you into any kind of risky situation is a boy who doesn't deserve to be put up with. Just because someone may have paid for your hamburger or because you have agreed to go out with him, doesn't make you in any way obligated to sit through a truly threatening time.

If, on the other hand, you find yourself in a position in which nothing particularly terrible has happened but you just don't feel good about what's going on, there may be some things that you can do about it.

If sitting and talking isn't working, you may want to suggest doing something else, like going to a game park or going skating or dancing. You don't have to talk on a date in order for it to be successful. In fact, sometimes situations in which you don't have to talk are much easier to feel comfortable in.

If you're in a bind, you may want to say something about what's going on. You might say, "I don't know about you, but I feel kind of nervous," or "Do you want to start this from the beginning again? I think I'll do better another time around." If you do dare to come right out and say something, be careful not to make it sound like you're blaming the bad time on the boy you're with (even if you do feel it's mostly his fault). Sharing the responsibility for the experience is the best way to take the pressure off both of you. In truth, whether or not two people are interacting successfully, it is a "responsibility" shared by both.

If nothing works and you come to the conclusion that the situation is hopeless, you've got the choice to either bear with it knowing that it will soon be over or to politely find a way of saying you have to leave early. Don't cut the evening off conspicuously early, however. Even if the boy you're with is dull and boring, that's still not reason enough to hurt his feelings. Say you've got homework or that you're not feeling well. And when you do get home, try not to be too discouraged. You are bound to have other dates that will be much more successful.

How Do Blind Dates Work?

A blind date is when two people get together who have never met each other before. Usually they have a friend in common, or some other connection through a relative or an acquaintance. Almost always, the people are referred to each other on someone else's recommendation. Maybe the son of an aunt's best friend is stopping over in your town on his way somewhere else. Your aunt may ask you to go out with him while he's visiting since he doesn't know anyone and you are both around the same age. She may not know him, but simply be asking you to do her a favor. That's a very blind date. Or else maybe an old friend from camp is also friendly with a boy whom she thinks you would like. Perhaps it's some interest you have in common or a similar approach to life in general, or else simply that she likes him, but she's involved with another boy. There are lots of ways blind dates can happen and as many ways as you can respond to them.

It's not a hard and fast rule, but it is a courtesy, when someone has an idea to set two people up together, to consult with the two people beforehand.

You can expect a call or a request on the order of, "I know this nice boy who I think you'd get along with; is it all right if I give him your number?" Usually the person who's doing the arranging will volunteer some information about the boy, especially if it's to his or her best interest that you go out with each other. If they don't, there's no reason you can't ask. But remember, it's only a date, so you don't need to know that much. Also, choose your questions according to who's doing the recommending. You might ask your best friend what he looks like, but maybe not your great aunt.

Chances are, no matter how you find out, you'll only hear about your date's good points, and there's always the possibility that even those are exaggerated. Actually, it's perfectly understandable. The referral person will probably have loyalty to both you and the boy in question. It's natural that he or she would want to at least encourage the two of you to see each other and at best contribute to having it work out well. And besides, most people in a situation like this would avoid giving you any information that might prejudice you against the person. So be prepared to hear great recommendations and take them for what they're worth.

The only thing to watch out for in a situation like this is the possibility that after hearing only a description of the boy, you get the impression that he is the boy of your dreams. The more questions you ask and the more positive replies you get, the greater the chance that you might think that. And if you are especially lonesome or eager to get involved with someone, your chances of expecting a lot are increased even more. So that's why you should try to control your expectations. Otherwise you're liable to be disappointed. Also, there are certain questions you may want to save to ask the boy directly. It's often more interesting and telling to see how a person presents himself than to hear him described by someone else.

The Idea Of A Blind Date Makes Me Nervous.

But what if you are in conflict about going out on the date at all? Try to understand what it might be that's making you afraid. Ask yourself a few questions. Is it that you feel uncomfortable meeting new people in general? Is it that you don't particularly trust the judgment of the person who's doing the recommending? Are you involved with someone else and not looking to meet other boys? Or do you just not like the whole idea of blind dates? Think about your reasons for being hesitant, and then decide if they are legitimate. You have no obligation to say yes, but remember that if you say no, you might be missing out on a nice time and the opportunity to get to know a nice or interesting person. If, after some thought, you decide you will do it, but you still feel slightly uneasy about the whole thing, you can say yes and then suggest a brief visit, such as grabbing a snack somewhere, that might not put you on the spot as much. You could also ask the boy if he'd like to go out with a group of your friends or drop by your house to listen to records. You might feel more comfortable on familiar turf.

What Kind of Problems Might I Have On A Blind Date?

Blind dates, once you're on them, can be a little harder than ordinary dates. In the first place, you're meeting with someone you've never spent any time with before, and in the beginning that's always a little difficult for anyone. Then there's the problem of what to talk about. You can talk about the friend you have in common, but that probably won't last you very long. If you're at a loss for what to say and the boy you're with seems to be having problems too, ask him some questions about himself. It's always interesting to find out about how another person lives, how their school might be different from your school, what it's like to live in the city, say, as opposed to the country, etc. If you are sincerely interested and you show it in the way you listen and respond, just a couple of questions can help a boy to open up to you and might also result in your learning that there are areas that the two of you have in common.

On the other hand, if you're both feeling uneasy, it might help to say so. Simply acknowledging the discomfort sometimes can make it go away. You might want to say, "Blind dates are weird, aren't they?" Or, "I was really nervous about meeting you." Or, "I've never been on a blind date and I didn't know what to expect." Most people appreciate honesty. If nothing else, you can laugh about how awkward you feel.

The best advice is probably to remind yourself that there's not much to lose by going on a blind date. At the very worst, you'll find yourself in not the most comfortable or fun situation. And at the very best, you could meet someone who you become very fond of.

Romantic RELATIONSHIPS

Beginning a relationship isn't hard. When an attraction between two people is mutual, a relationship often seems to just naturally develop. It's maintaining a good relationship that's difficult. Sometimes it may feel like you have no control over your relationship at all. Other times it can be as simple as taking the time to sit and think about what it means to you to be involved romantically with another person. Even the most experienced couples struggle with this.

A relationship can be a wonderful and supportive addition to your life. But like anything really worth having, it takes some work. If you make time to consider what you and your partner need in the relationship, and what you can give to it, you should find the rough spots getting a little less rough.

Caring enough to think about the other person's feelings, and to look at yourself objectively, can lead to a very meaningful experience.

What Do I Want From One Anyway?

It's likely you'll find that you'll want different things from a relationship depending on who you're involved with and how you feel about him. Your age and past experiences will also make a difference. And probably, if you're in a romantic relationship for a long period of time, what you need from it will change, since as you grow your perspective on things will change and shift constantly.

It's a good idea to sometimes stop and think about exactly how you feel. Does the person you're with give you what you think you want? Is it realistic to expect everything you would ideally like? Does what you want affect your boyfriend and the relationship in general?

It's helpful sometimes to discuss these different feelings with the person you're involved with. While it's nice to think that these kind of things should be understood and not have to be spelled out, it's not always so clear in a relationship, especially if you yourself aren't quite sure of how you feel. Talking can help to sort out your own feelings and also give you a better idea of just what your partner feels and wants, too. If a boy doesn't know what you want, he won't be able to give it to you.

What If The Things I Want Keep Changing?

In the beginning, you may want a boy you're interested in simply to like you. Probably, you'll also want him to find you pretty. If a relationship develops, you'll begin to want other things as well. As with a friend, you may want to be able to talk and feel understood by this boy. Maybe you'll want him to be available to listen to you whenever you've got something to talk about that concerns you. Perhaps you'll want to count on him to be with you every weekend, or to do something special with you on your vacation. You could want him to be completely honest with you or to tell you everywhere he goes. When you're feeling sick, you may expect him to comfort you. When you're feeling sad, you may depend on him to cheer you up. Maybe from your boyfriend, you expect a nightly call or presents on special occasions.

In a more general way, you'll want to feel appreciated, that you're with someone who understands you like no one else does, and that your boyfriend is someone you could trust.

There's nothing wrong with wanting any of these things or even all of them. In fact, it's natural to expect a lot from a romantic relationship. By the time we're teenagers, we've seen so many movies and read so many books about love, that usually most of us have already conjured up a detailed picture of what love should be for us and maybe even what a loved one should look like.

Fantasizing is fun, and wishing for something you want very badly is, too. The only risk is in being too rigid, expecting to get everything you want or even insisting on it. It's possible to get so caught up in worrying about what you want that you find you've forgotten to take the other person's feelings into consideration. You may think you're sure you know what love should be, but in actual practice it may turn out to be something altogether different. That can make you very angry. But just because it's different than you expected doesn't mean it's bad. Maybe your wishes or needs conflict with those of your boyfriend. If you can't be flexible, you're sure to have problems.

Relationships are funny. They can make you

feel more secure and at home than anything else does. You can feel that in your relationship you are more yourself than you are anywhere else. But relationships can also make you feel unfamiliar and strange. They can make you feel cheerful when you thought you'd feel sad, or distant from a partner when you hoped you'd feel close. It may seem confusing, but in each of these experiences there's something to learn. If you're open-minded enough, and try hard not to worry about what a relationship *should be* but to see what yours *is*, you may find happy surprises and unexpected pleasures, and uncover some important things about yourself you never knew before.

Am I In It For The Right Or The Wrong Reasons?

It's hard to say what constitutes a good relationship or what makes one bad. What might be good for one person might not be very good for another.

But when it comes to the reasons a person gets involved, some are clearly better than others. That's not to say that a relationship started for the wrong reasons can't become a good relationship, or that a relationship started for all the right reasons can't eventually turn sour. All it means is that it's sometimes good to stop and think about why you're getting involved with a person. This is especially important when there's the chance that you may be doing it less because of how you feel about him, and more because of some of the unsure things you feel about yourself. There are many feelings and circumstances that might lead you to enter a relationship for the wrong reasons:

●Getting involved with a boy because everybody else is involved with one and you feel funny without one.

●Getting involved with a boy because he's pressuring you and it's easier than saying no all the time.

●Getting involved with a boy simply because you think you're too old to be without one.

●Getting involved, or staying involved, because you're lonely or afraid of being alone.

●Getting involved with a boy only because everybody wants to be involved with him and you'd feel like a jerk if you didn't.

●Getting involved because your friend says he's perfect for you.

●Staying involved because you're afraid of what he'd do if you left.

●Staying involved because it's easier than getting to know someone new.

On the other hand, there are many good feelings you can experience that might signal a great relationship is ahead:

•Getting involved because you feel comfortable and enjoy just being around the person.

•Getting involved because you appreciate what makes that person unique and he appreciates what makes you unique.

•Getting involved because something about him just makes you smile a lot.

•Getting involved because you love his sense of humor.

•Getting involved because you truly care about what happens to each other.

•Getting involved because you have a lot of interests in common with each other.

•Staying involved because you are encouraging each other to do the best you can do at whatever you want to.

•Staying involved because you are nice to each other and most of the time feel good around each other.

How Can I Improve A Relationship?

All relationships can use improving, no matter how good they might be. Sometimes they improve on their own without either of the two people feeling like they've had to make an effort at all. Most of the time, to make the relationship they are in better, people have to try.

Improving a relationship takes time, trust, sensitivity, and the ability for both people to admit to themselves and each other when they think they are wrong. A relationship in which one person stubbornly holds his or her position and never stops to consider the other person's side is a relationship that won't grow, and growing in a relationship is what is meant by improving. Likewise, a relationship in which two people are dishonest with one another or otherwise unable to trust each other is one in which there's a shaky foundation to build on.

If you're in a relationship that means a lot to you but may not always be going as well as you'd like it to, try to think about the areas that you believe could use improvement. Maybe your relationship isn't as honest and open as you wish it could be. Is it because you don't trust your boyfriend enough to open up to him? Are you afraid he may not still like you once he hears about how you *really* feel? Do you hold back some of your feelings because your boyfriend does, or are you holding back because of your own fears?

Probably the hardest part of improving a relationship is the honesty part. Not only is it hard to be honest, especially when admitting to things you might be ashamed of, but it's also hard to know when to be honest. Honesty can hurt as much as it can help a relationship. And if it's not used sensitively, it can be taken as criticism. That's why if there is something bothering you about your relationship or, specifically, something bothering you about the way your boyfriend behaves, sometimes the best way to handle it is to talk about how you feel rather than about what's wrong with the way things are. If you can avoid making judgments and instead talk strictly about feelings, you'll probably get better results. You may even find your boyfriend expressing more of his own feelings in the process. The most effective way to get another person to open up is to open up yourself.

That goes for trust, too. You can't make someone more trustworthy, but you can encourage them simply by being trustworthy yourself. Are you somebody your boyfriend can rely on to keep your word, keep his secrets, and care for him? Sometimes developing trust is just a matter of every once and a while showing someone how much they mean to you. Everybody has their own way of doing that, and sometimes even the littlest gesture can help to make someone feel more secure in a relationship.

If something about your boyfriend is particularly irritating and you think talking about it could improve your relationship, broach the subject carefully. Nobody likes to feel that someone else is trying to change them. It could make someone feel as if you don't really like them the way they are. Try to mix your criticism with compliments. Think of an incident when your boyfriend acted in a way that made you feel particularly good and use that as an example when talking about something that may be bothering you. You could say something on the order of, "You made me feel so much better the other day when you included me in the conversation with your friend, but other times, like today, I felt so out of it. I need you to help me feel more a part of the group."

If you've done something that hurt your boyfriend, apologize, even if he hasn't come out and said he's angry at you. A quick acknowledgment of something hurtful you've done doesn't excuse it, but does sometimes make the pain go away faster. If you find you're apologizing a lot, particularly about the same kind of behavior, maybe you should also stop and look at what you're doing and think about ways that you might be able to change it.

Take time every once in a while to talk about what's good about what you have together. You may be taking a lot of what's good for granted, or forgetting in the fights or everyday routines exactly what brought you together in the first place. A good relationship is something for both people to be proud of. The fact that there are so many positive things between you is good reason to celebrate. After all, you both contribute to making it what it is; why not share the credit for it too?

Learn to laugh together, and keep in mind the things you can do to make your boyfriend laugh. Everybody takes things too seriously at some point or another. Sometimes a good laugh can help you both realize that, whatever the problem, it wasn't really as terribly serious as you thought.

Try to do as many diverse and interesting things together as you can. It will enhance your relationship and give you fond memories of times you enjoyed together.

How Do I Know When It's Wrong?

When you're in the middle of a relationship, it's hard to know whether it's right or wrong for you. If it were all one or the other, things might be easier, or if it were possible to be objective things might be clearer. But in a close relationship, objectivity and logic are pretty difficult to come by.

That's why it sometimes helps to know the warning signals that indicate the relationship is not one that you should stay in:

•If you're in a lot of pain over your relationship, if you find you're often or regularly crying over something that keeps happening with you and your partner.

•If, after a considerable amount of time, you still don't feel comfortable or secure enough around your boyfriend to openly express your feelings.

•If the boy you're with talks only about himself, is only interested in things *he* wants to do, and only wants to see you when he's ready.

•If you find you're often disappointed, either in terms of expecting things and not getting them, or often wishing things would be different than they are.

•If you're sure you like your boyfriend a lot more than he likes you.

•If you don't believe many of the things your boyfriend tells you.

•If you find that a lot of the time you can't enjoy yourself around your boyfriend.

•If you're always fighting, and making up is delayed and often difficult.

•If you can't think of why you're in it.

•If you don't like yourself in the relationship, if you see yourself behaving in a way that's not the most flattering to you, if you're in bad moods a lot, whiney, overly critical, and generally feeling ugly.

Is There Such A Thing As Getting Out Of A Relationship Gracefully?

It might be impossible to get out of a relationship painlessly, but it shouldn't be impossible to get out of it gracefully. If you've been hurt or if you are confused about whether or not you should be leaving in the first place, it's difficult to deal with things smoothly. Either way, and whatever the cause of your break up, you'll probably feel much better afterwards if you can handle it in as graceful and dignified a way as you can manage.

The gist of it is to avoid certain pitfalls.

•Don't simply stop calling your boyfriend or suddenly ignore him. That's cruel and irresponsible.

•Don't have someone else tell him for you.

•Don't just pick up and start seeing someone else and expect your boyfriend to figure it out for himself.

•Don't, no matter how angry you are, break up

with complaints of everything you've always hated about him but never told him before. It's too late to do anything about it now, so why bother?

●Don't set someone up with him and hope that she'll solve your problems of getting him away from you.

●Don't rehash bitterness for any length of time—unless of course you don't actually intend to break up but are just using it as a threat (that in itself isn't very graceful).

●Don't have a physical fight over it. With emotions flying, you could get hurt.

●Don't spread nasty stories about your boyfriend. It's spiteful and mean and another way of having other people do your dirty work.

●Don't simply refuse to see your boyfriend or not answer his calls.

Then What Is A Nice Way To Break Up?

It won't be easy, and therefore it's good to be prepared. Once you've decided that breaking up is what you want to do, then try to think of an appropriate way and place to do it. It's romantic to pick a place that was always a favorite place for the two of you, but any reminders of better times together could just make the breakup more painful. You'll probably want privacy, but not too much. Anything that will make it tempting to get back into old familiar routines will only make it harder for the two of you. Pick a neutral place like a park bench or a quiet booth in a restaurant where you know you won't see people you know. You don't want to memorize a speech but you may want to at least review what you are going to say. Try to include in it at least some mention of the good qualities in your relationship, but don't get carried away or mushy; the message in that would only be confusing.

If you feel you were partly responsible for the breakup, say so. Give some reasons. But don't feel you have to give all. You know why you're getting out of it, but you don't have to share it all with him. If you think it will be hard for him and know it will be hard for you, too, admit it. That's one way of saying the relationship was meaningful to you despite the fact that you also know it can't continue.

How Do I Cope With The Hurt Of A Breakup?

More often than not when a relationship breaks up, it's not mutual. No matter what someone may tell you, almost everyone has had the experience of their boyfriend or girlfriend either ending, or changing the intensity of, a relationship. It doesn't take much to know that it feels bad. Imagine losing a close friend or a member of your family. You would have a great sense of loss, and feelings of loneliness, sadness, and maybe even anger.

When someone you've been attached to leaves you, it can be so painful that you could feel like you'll never be able to get over him or the pain of the experience. It might cause you to play back in your mind all the good times you had together, and that could make you miss your boyfriend even more. Breaking up could also make you behave in a way that's not typical for you. You might try to convince the boy to stay with you, a move which ordinarily you'd be too proud to consider. Your moods could be subject to quick changes, and your friends might find it difficult to get along with you.

Basically, if the boy you've been with wants to end the relationship, for whatever reasons, at some point you're going to have to come to terms with that. If you are full with feelings that you want to express, and know that talking to your boyfriend won't help, you may want to start a journal. It can give you an outlet for your feelings and an opportunity to understand them better. You might also want to talk to a friend. A good friend can offer you comfort and maybe some insights you yourself hadn't thought of.

You may also want to, at least temporarily, try to keep yourself a little busier than usual. It won't solve your problems, but it can help to distract you from them. Sports can help you take your mind off the breakup and release the tension that might be building up because of it. Creative activities are a good outlet, too. Pick an activity that takes concentration, and you'll find it provides a sort of vacation from the bad feelings you've been unable to escape. The more you do, the more you should come to appreciate that, while your relationship was an important part of your life, it was only one part. You are still a complete person without it.

Can We Be Just Friends?

Some people can, and some people can't. Whether or not you can stay friends after you've broken up with someone you've been romantically involved with depends a lot on what your relationship was like in the first place, and on exactly how you broke up.

Obviously, if a boy you were close to simply

stops calling, or leaves you by switching to a friend of yours, you'll feel hurt. It will take either a lot of time or a later confrontation in which your ex-boyfriend faces up to it like a true friend, before you can feel friendly towards him again.

If there wasn't at least some agreement in the breakup, if one of you definitely wanted it and the other definitely didn't, that probably will also take some time before you can be friends again.

The question of staying friends usually comes up when two people have mixed feelings about separating in the first place. Many relationships end this way. You and your boyfriend may both know that it just can't work, but maybe there are good things about the relationship that you're not ready to give up. Or else, maybe you both know it's wrong to stay with each other, but neither of you wants to face being alone again. Maybe it's easier to stay together in some form, at least until each of you gets into a new relationship.

Staying friends can seem like a solution. But it can also, if not dealt with sensitively, become a problem. To begin with, it may be difficult to establish the boundaries of friendship with someone you've previously been romantically involved with. Can you expect the same things from one another? Is your relationship unchanged except for the fact that you won't be physical anymore? What does it mean, then, if you find yourself by accident getting physical again after you've officially broken up? As friends, do you have less responsibility to one another than you did when you were romantically involved? Are you to call each other less, or share fewer of your feelings with each other?

While it can be satisfying to stay friends with someone you've been romantic with, to do so after a breakup it can sometimes also be confusing. The new terms of the relationship you try to establish might not be so easy to follow. Once you've been in a specific role with another person, it's often hard to switch into another one. Just because you've broken up with a boy doesn't mean you'll suddenly stop being jealous of his interests in other girls. If you're used to daily phone calls from your boyfriend, when the frequency diminishes, it will feel strange. No matter what you call your relationship, the new arrangement will be something that you'll have to get used to.

You may also as "just friends" find that there are times, maybe when you're feeling lonely or especially close to one another, that you act like boyfriend and girlfriend again. Nothing is particularly wrong with that in and of itself. In fact, it's very natural for people who've once been intimate to feel attracted to each other sometimes long after they've broken up. The problem is that it could be harder to accept the breakup once you get back into old routines. If breaking up is what you both want, putting it off or "temporarily" ignoring it will only extend the pain.

Sometimes within the new context of friendship two people who were once involved with each other romantically come to appreciate each other even more than they did when they were together. Maybe they miss each other and take that to mean they ought to be together. Without the pressure and responsibilities of the relationship, they can feel more relaxed with one another.

Often it takes a few breakups and reconciliations before two people can decide whether or not they should stay together. Usually they realize they shouldn't if after making up they find themselves quickly falling back into the old problems that were the reason for their separation to begin with.

Though it's rare, it is possible to experience a breakup that's relatively friendly and clear cut. When two people agree that it's better to separate, they often can part with warm feelings and the recognition that they had a special attachment and appreciation for one another. Sometimes if they were friends before they got romantically involved, they have a better chance of being friends afterwards. A breakup then is a recognition that while they may be friends, they can't necessarily be good romantic partners. In a situation like that, the friendship can still remain intact.

But often, whatever the circumstance, when two people break up they need time apart from each other to sort out exactly what happened and to recover from the pain of it. If you want to be friends but your ex-boyfriend is too hurt, respect his position. He may need more time than you do to get over what happened between you. It might be good for you to get a distance from it, too. Just because you can't be friends immediately doesn't mean it can't happen eventually. Sometimes it happens weeks later, sometimes months. If enough time has passed and each of you have found ways to heal your wounds, you may make it as friends after all.

SEXUALITY

Nobody needs to tell you that your body is changing now. You probably notice new things about yourself often just looking in the mirror. Maybe you notice the difference most in friends. Someone who for years has been around your height may have recently grown so much that she is now taller than you. Another's breasts may have grown much larger than yours are. Everyone changes at their own rate. That has more to do with heredity than anything else. And most young people aren't easily satisfied with the changes as they take place. One teenage boy may think he's growing too fast. Another may worry that he's not growing fast enough. Maybe you haven't gotten your period yet but your best friend has. That could make you feel impatient for yours.

Mostly, puberty is a hard thing to get used to. This is the time during which your body arrives at sexual maturity, anywhere generally between the ages of ten and eighteen. Is your skin getting oily, your chest getting bigger?; are you growing hair where you never had it before? No matter how normal the changes you're going through happen to be, just the fact that your appearance is changing so dramatically is enough to make you feel unsure of yourself. Maybe you're also feeling sensations you've never felt before. That can be overwhelming, too.

Knowing a little bit more about what's going on may ease some of this discomfort, or at least help you realize that some of the strange things you're feeling are really normal and very natural. The fact is that there are very logical reasons for why your body is changing the way it is now and real physical reasons for why, as a teenager you may be experiencing a lot of new feelings.

What Is Puberty?

In very simple terms, puberty means the time when a girl's or boy's body becomes ready to conceive children. In boys that means the ability to produce sperm and in girls that means the ability to produce eggs, or ova. Without both, babies cannot be made.

But, of course, boys and girls are different from one another for more reasons than that. Now is the time when, physically at least, those differences become most apparent. The main difference or the main reason for the difference is that girls or women, unlike men, can carry and bear children. It's why girls/women have more fat in their bodies than boys (in order to cushion the body so that it can protect a developing fetus from injury); it's why girls/women have larger hips (to allow for the passage of a baby out of the body); and why women have larger breasts than men do (to produce milk to feed a newborn).

But what about all the other things going on in your body now, the things not as obvious to other people but very obvious to you? Does oily skin have anything to do with having babies? Does perspiring a lot? What about that tingling feeling you may get when you're around a boy you may like, or your dramatic shifts in moods? It may not seem related but a good part of it really is.

These kind of changes take place primarily because of high levels of sex hormones that your body is producing now that you're a teenager. A hormone is a chemical. When released in your bloodstream it acts as a kind of messenger to other parts of your body. In boys, hormones are produced in the testicles. In girls, they are produced deeper inside the body in the ovaries. At the onset of puberty a part of your brain called the hypothalamus activates the production of hormones. It's as if an alarm goes off in your brain signaling the rest of your body to begin the process of sexual maturity. That's why it may seem like so much is going on at once. It *is* going on at once, and it's affecting your body in visible as well as invisible ways. Hormones can affect your hair and your skin and sometimes even your moods, and because they're in such quantity now they may be giving you a heightened feeling of sexual sensation.

What Am I Like On The Inside?

Unlike in the male anatomy, girl's reproductive organs are mostly on the inside. The vaginal opening is like an entranceway to them. If you've explored your own body or seen pictures, you probably know that the vagina stops not very far up inside of you, usually just a few inches. At the end of the vaginal canal is something that feels like the tip of your nose. It's called the cervix, and is the opening to your uterus or womb. The uterus is where a fetus grows when it is developing in woman's body. In the middle of the cervix is a small opening or hole. It is through this opening that sperm can travel when a man ejaculates into a woman during intercourse. It is also through this hole that the menstrual blood is expelled each month when a woman has her period.

On either side of the uterus are the ovaries. That's where a woman's eggs are developed and from where, each month, they are released. Connecting the ovaries to the uterus are two tubes (one on either side) called the Fallopian tubes. Each month at least one egg is released (sometimes two or more, leading to possible multiple births) down one tube; then the next month, another egg is released from the other tube. Ovulation occurs about halfway into a girl's/woman's menstrual cycle. Since the average length between one period and another is twenty-eight days, ovulation is figured to occur on or around the fourteenth day of the cycle. It is the time when a woman is fertile, the time when the egg is matured and in a position to be fertilized. It is the time a woman can become pregnant if her egg is fertilized by sperm.

If the egg isn't fertilized, it is expelled approximately fourteen days later, along with the fluids that have accumulated in the uterus as preparation for a developing fetus. This is called menstruation. It can last anywhere from one to seven days.

Sexual Urges: What Do I Make Of Them?

Maybe one of the reasons there's so much written about sex, so much spoken about it, and so many arguments about the wrong or right of it, is that sexual feelings can be very powerful. And because they are such strong feelings, they can be very confusing at times.

While sex and sexual feelings are a basic integrated part of a person's experience, it doesn't always feel like that. Sexual feelings can come to you at the most unexpected times. They can come over you like a wave and then go away again, sometimes leaving you feeling that whatever happened, happened from somewhere outside of yourself. Actually, sexual feelings, just like any other feelings, don't come from anywhere on the outside but belong somewhere deep down inside of you. They're private feelings. And they're your feelings to decide what to do with.

As you grow, your sexual feelings will develop. They'll change with you as your feelings change and as you move through various stages in your life. At this point in your life they may feel like a lot to keep up with, and pretty scary sometimes, too. But that's because the feelings are so new. As you get more used to them, you'll get more secure with them.

Is It Natural To Be Afraid To Touch?

Sometimes it's hard to know whether or not to act on your attraction for someone no matter how strong it might be. You can find yourself in what can seem like a no-win situation. Maybe you're not sure how you feel about a boy. You know you're attracted to him and you know you like being with him, but you don't know if you want to get any closer to him than you already are. He may be pushing you to be more physically involved with him, or be growing impatient if you're not. You may know of other people your age who talk of sex as though it's a regular, common, everyday activity, but to you it feels like something more serious. Just kissing or touching may make you feel a little uncomfortable, especially if it's with someone you don't know very well. Also, if you've never been close that way to someone else before, it can be a little frightening or at least awkward. Even if you've had experience, you might feel uneasy. You may want to be sure that the boy likes you for the right reasons, or else you simply may feel like you want to be close to him in other ways before he touches you in such a personal way. And what if you kiss a little and then the boy wants more?

Does Kissing Lead To Intercourse?

Kissing, hugging, touching, and holding someone whom you like close to you is all part of sex. Some people say it's the best part because it's through these kinds of actions that you can express the most feeling. Other people may say that it's only a prelude to intercourse and that without intercourse it's only frustrating. But kissing, hugging, and touching are important in their own right, and don't need anything else to feel good or be good. In your teen years these kinds of ways of being sexual can also help you learn about your body and the body of whomever you're with. In a slow, easy way it allows you to explore your sensations and learn about what feels good to each of you. It also, if taken slowly, can give you the kind of time you might need to figure out how you feel. It *is* possible to be intimate without being intense. In that way, hugging and kissing and touching can be an outlet for you to express gentle, friendly feelings toward another person.

What Happens When My Physical Feelings Grow Strong?

You might be satisfied making out for hours with your boyfriend without feeling at all frustrated. Your sexual sensations feel lovely and calm. On the other hand, you may feel frustrated but know that you don't want to get closer physically than you already are. The feelings could be too strong or too frightening for you. Usually, simply stopping what you're doing and taking a deep breath is enough to calm yourself down. (That goes for both boys and girls.)

But sometimes without even thinking about it, sexual feelings can suddenly become very strong. Just kissing could make you or the person you're with feel like you need or want more. On a physical level, it's natural for sexual feelings to build up. As a person's body is stimulated sexually, or aroused, it tends to feel pleasurably tense and excited. These sensations can grow so powerful that the body seeks release from the excited feelings. This release is called an orgasm, and most everyone enjoys them when they happen.

It's important to know, however, that you don't need an orgasm to enjoy being physically close with someone. The good physical and emotional feelings you get from kissing and touching can be wonderful all by themselves.

If I'm Not Ready For More Serious Sex, Will A Boy Drop Me?

There are lots of good reasons that you might not want to get too physically involved with a boy. Maybe you're simply very attracted to someone who you know is absolutely wrong for you. Maybe he's involved with someone else, dishonest, irresponsible, or not especially nice to you in general. Your better judgment may tell you he's not the boy for you, but sexually you may feel drawn to him. Maybe you like a boy very much but you just don't feel comfortable enough or ready to get so close. It can be a difficult spot to be in.

Sometimes the best way to handle a situation like this is to remind yourself that despite how you might feel, it is not urgent. You don't have to decide what you want to do immediately. If a boy can't wait for you to make up your mind or isn't patient or sensitive enough to take your feelings into consideration, that doesn't mean anything's wrong with you. Whether or not you want to get closer is your prerogative. Or if you're not sure of someone, you can always wait until you have a better idea about what you might want. You have every right to take as long as you need to decide, or, after it all, to decide that it's something you don't want.

You also have every right to change your mind. Just because you may have gotten sexual with someone doesn't make you obligated to keep being sexual with him. And this is true about everything from kissing to intercourse.

Basically, it's hard to know and hard to decide, especially these days when there's so much pressure to conform to what everybody else at least seems to be doing. And there are no simple answers that can necessarily make any of this easier for you. Talking to someone else can help. An older person who's already considered these questions can often offer insights that you might not yet have arrived at. Some girls like to talk to their mothers. Others sometimes pick an older person they admire. It may help you to simply talk to a friend, particularly if you can be honest about your confused feelings. It can also help to speak openly with the person in question.

The decision to have more involved sexual relationships may be your own, but a sexual experience is a shared experience. What you feel about it is as important as what you do about it. If nothing more, just discussing those feelings can make you closer and more comfortable with the person you care about.

Do I Need To Be Experienced To Enjoy Being Close?

Because there's so much talk about sexuality these days, there are also a lot of misconceptions around about it. One of the biggest of those misconceptions is that there is a technique to being sexual and lessons or rules you can follow that can make you sexier than you are already. So new books come out professing to have the answer to becoming a good lover, and many people buy them because everyone wants to be one.

But what happens when two people are intimate is not something that can be taught. A person could be familiar with all the principals of good kissing, for example, and still not enjoy kissing. That's because to be *good* at kissing is basically to *feel* good about kissing, and all the lessons in the world can't teach someone that.

Still, at some point in yours and everyone else's life, a situation may come up in which, faced with the possibility of being intimate with another person, you worry that you may not be experienced enough. You may fear you won't know enough to make the encounter really nice.

However nervous you may be, it usually, in the right kind of situation, doesn't take long for you to realize that there actually isn't very much to worry about at all. If someone likes you, and feels attracted to you, they will probably enjoy being close to you no matter what you do. And similarly, if you like someone else, and come to feel comfortable with him, you'll find yourself easily expressing those feelings in a relaxed, physical way. So it's not really what you do that matters, it's how you feel about what you're doing, and who you're doing it with.

But What If I'm Out With A More Experienced Older Person?

If you're worried about not knowing what to do, if you're going out with someone who's a little older than you are, the best advice is to remember that the person you're with won't decide he doesn't like you because of something you just don't feel ready for. Those aren't the kind of things that matter when it comes to real love, romance, or friendship. Everyone deserves patience and understanding, and you have a right to just that. It's fair to assume the person you are with already likes you, or you wouldn't be alone with him. And you probably like him, too.

The other thing that would help, is to make a conscious effort to relax. Sometimes it can be as simple as taking a very deep breath and reminding yourself that your date may, in fact, be as nervous as you are. Experience doesn't automatically bring confidence! Other times it helps to say you're nervous or even to go so far as saying why you're nervous. Granted, it's hard to admit to these kinds of feelings, but sometimes simply expressing them will ease the tension.

What Are The Physical Risks Involved With Intercourse?

Sex education is on the curriculum of most phys-ed classes. Newspapers and magazines carry articles on intimacy, and because there's so much discussion about the risks of being sexually active, it's assumed that by their teen years most young people know what's at stake when they decide to have sex.

You too have probably gotten the point. From sex you can get pregnant or you can contract a number of serious infections.

These aren't reasons enough to abstain from sex, but they are important things to know if you should decide to have it. There aren't a lot of facts to learn. But sometimes just knowing them isn't enough. Unless you can *do* something about what you know, you are no better off than if you know nothing at all.

It takes more than knowing the facts to be cautious. In sex, it takes believing that it can happen to you, that you can get pregnant or contract a venereal disease and that because you're young or healthy or both, you are not necessarily immune to any of these things. The next step is knowing why you wouldn't want any of it to happen to you.

Pregnancy

The fact is, it's hard to simply comprehend pregnancy, no matter how much you might know about the reproductive system. It is equally hard to imagine what it would be like for you personally to be pregnant. Because pregnancy is imbued with such strong emotions and many colorful and romantic associations, it's also something that's hard for anyone to completely reject. Most girls and women have probably at one time or another dreamt about being pregnant and having a baby. In a culture like ours that makes so much of motherhood, it's hard not to. So pregnancy is also a hard thing to be sure about not wanting.

While having a baby when you're ready can be a wonderful thing, at the wrong time it can be a big problem. It is taxing physically, emotionally, and financially. And for a young person, those added pressures are often hardest to bear.

The teen years are at a time of considerable emotional and physical growth. Getting pregnant during that time can sap a person of energy that would otherwise be used for the hard enough tasks of growing up, school responsibilities, and career plans. Physically, most teenagers can endure pregnancy. Our bodies have evolved in such a way that they make us ready to become pregnant at an early age. But a lot of teenagers are not mentally or emotionally prepared to be parents. Certain adults may not be either. Altogether, it's hard to deal with the responsibility for another human life no matter what your circumstance. But for a teenager, whose life is in turmoil and transition to begin with, having a baby is an especially risky experience. Many people who've had children at a very young age regret it afterwards, no matter how much they might love their child. They speak of how their lives dramatically changed once their children were born and how they feel they missed out on an important part of their lives. Some feel they could have been much better mothers were they older, and that their children suffered from their lack of maturity.

But happily, if you know you don't want to get pregnant just yet, there are very real, simple, and effective precautions you can take.

Birth Control

If you are thinking of having sex, or have had sex already unprotected, make an appointment to see a gynecologist. Most towns have their own chapter of Planned Parenthood. Look in your phone book for the number. If someone there can't see you, they will refer you to someone who can. If you have a relative you can speak openly with, ask him or her for a recommendation. Try asking your school nurse, if you feel comfortable enough with him or her to speak confidentially. Ideally, a gynecologist should be someone to whom you can ask questions, and speak of your concerns. He or she can help educate you as to how to best take care of your body.

There are more reasons to go to a gynecologist than simply to get birth control or to be treated for an illness. A lot of women visit a gynecologist regularly as a form of good preventative health care. Doctors are by profession supposed to be objective. Even though it might feel embarrassing, if you do see a doctor, try to be as open as you can about anything that might be worrying you. They are there to help you, but can't do that unless they know what's on your mind.

The doctor can also help you make a decision about birth control.

Basically, there are four types of birth control available today.

The first kind stops the sperm from traveling freely up through the cervix to meet the egg. The condom, diaphragm, and cervical cap, serve this purpose.

The second kind kills the sperm before they can reach the egg. Foam, spermicidal jellies, spermicidal suppositories are the effective agents.

The third kind, the IUD, interferes with conception by physically affecting the state of the cervix and uterus.

The fourth kind, the pill, through chemicals or artificial hormones inhibits normal ovulation.

All work to some degree, though some are better than others. Some people use a few methods at a time just to make sure not to get pregnant. Others change from one to another because their relationships change their habits, their body, or their preferences. None of the methods work if they are not followed as per instruction.

Venereal Disease

Anyone can get VD, and anyone can pass it on. All it takes is one sexual contact. And once you've got it, it won't go away until it is treated. Venereal disease is not a reason not to have sex, but it certainly is enough of a reason to be careful and cautious. It is more widespread now than ever before.

There are recognizable signs. A male may experience discomfort with urination, and a yellowish discharge from the penis. In a woman the disease is unfortunately more difficult to recognize, as most times the symptoms are invisible. If your boyfriend has or suspects he has VD, encourage him to go to the doctor for tests and treatment. There are a number of strains of VD; many require different sorts of medication. Make sure you find out from your boyfriend what strain he has, and go to the doctor as well. Even if you are sure you do not have a venereal disease, but think your boyfriend does, you should have a culture test. Again, it is important to remember that just because you have no obvious signs, it does not mean you do not have the disease.

In most towns there are VD clinics where, at a minimal cost, they can test you and dispense medication if it should turn out you need it. Most forms of VD are easily cured. If you take your medication as prescribed, most venereal diseases will clear up within a period of a couple of weeks.

It is very important for your own and your boyfriend's physical and emotional well-being to try and keep an open line of communication. Your health could depend on it.

The Consequences of VD

Venereal diseases in all their forms are very serious infections. They are highly contagious. Once you've contracted one, it can spread to other parts of your body. Most venereal diseases don't, in their early stages, make you feel sick like you're used to feeling sick but while they're not hurting, they can do very serious damage to your internal organs if left untreated. In both men and women, having an untreated venereal disease for a lengthy period of time can lead to sterility. For people who eventually want to have children, not being able to is a very sad thing indeed.

Another concern for women in particular is venereal disease has recently been connected to another disease called pelvic inflammatory disease, or PID. Pelvic inflammatory disease is very serious. It is an acute infection of the pelvic area, and is painful and often requires hospitalization. PID, even when treated, often has damaging effects on a woman's reproductive organs, making it very hard for some women to have children afterwards. There are also some forms of venereal disease that have been linked to certain strains of cancer. It is not certain that there is a corollation but studies are showing that with women who've had a venereal disease called herpes simplex, there seems to be a higher incidence of cancer of the cervix later on.

Herpes is an annoying and sometimes painful

disease and one that is rapidly spreading. Unlike most other venereal diseases, there are no medicines yet on the market to prevent herpes disease or to completely cure it once you've got it. Some cases are worse than others, and while certainly at times the symptoms are quite bearable, it is a distressing disease both physically and emotionally. Both men and women can contract it, but with women the symptoms are generally more painful and could have more serious consequences. The most unfortunate thing about herpes is that once a person has it he or she is stuck with it. The painful symptoms often disappear for long periods of time, but the disease in a very mild form remains.

What Are The Emotional Risks?

While the physical risks in sex are the most obvious, there are other more subtle emotional risks a person takes when he or she decides to have sex. Though not physically threatening, these kinds of risks might call for just as much caution.

Depending on the situation, the relationship, and the state of mind a person might be in, sex can be everything from a dull to a highly charged emotional experience. But it rarely is simple. In a conversation between two people, each of their private lives, feelings, and desires affect what they say, and how they say it. The same is true of kissing and touching. It is a kind of conversation too, though for the most part, communication is non-verbal. A lot of silent thoughts and private feelings are going on. Take that and add on to it the most personal feelings two individuals have about their bodies, their conflicts between what they've been taught is right and what they feel is right, and all of the emotions that have brought them together in the first place, and you've got a loaded experience.

The thing about a sexual experience, though, is that it can sometimes happen easily and swiftly, and only when it is over do the complicated feelings really emerge.

When two people who don't know each other very well have sex with one another, they may feel afterwards that they know each other much better even though no words have passed between them. But it's a feeling that may not last.

Sex between two people who are not communicating with each other can be at least as frustrating and depressing as a conversation in which two people interrupt, ignore, or misunderstand one another. Except in sex there's more to misunderstand and more to ignore, and, on top of it all, a lot more expected than in a simple conversation. Since you've gotten as close as you can get with another person, it's easy to feel that now you should share everything, know everything, and be everything for each other. But there's a problem in that.

Sometimes two people come to sex with different expectations. One person may only be doing it for the fun and excitement it offers. The other might be getting into it for the feelings of love it brings to the surface and the opportunity to express affection. The aftermath of a sexual experience can be hurtful to the person expecting more than his or her partner wants to give. It can also be frightening.

Sometimes two people aren't prepared for the strong feelings intimacy can strike up. For two people ready to be with each other, the sharing can be a wonderful experience. But for others, not prepared for such closeness, it can be intimidating. Just because people can be physically close, does not in anyway mean they can handle each other's emotional needs. Too many demands can be scary.

Sex can stir up all sorts of emotions, depending on how you feel about yourself, your body, and the person you're involved with. At its best, it can make two people feel very good and close to one another. But because it can also bring to the surface conflicting emotions between people, it can be an alienating experience as well.

FRIENDS

There are many kinds of friends a person can have and many good reasons to have them. Each type of friend you have can serve different needs for you. You may talk to your best friend in a way you'd never talk to anyone else. One good friend might be your favorite person to play volleyball with. Another one might be someone who you feel most comfortable with just sitting around doing nothing.

But with each type of friendship also comes its own special set of problems. A good friend, whom you would expect to remember something like your birthday, might be forgetful. Another might be too attentive, to the point where all her calling and questions are beginning to annoy you. Your best friend and you might get along very well when you're alone with each other, but in a crowd, especially when there are boys around, you might not get along very well at all. What if one of your friends is also friendly with someone you dislike? What if a good friend of yours gets involved with a boy you recently broke up with? Can you stay friends with her then?

Friendships may be complicated, but when they work they can also be some of the most satisfying relationships in your life.

What Is A Good Friend Anyway?

Usually when two people like each other it's obvious from the start. Something draws you to the other person and them to you. In the beginning, at least, getting to know each other can feel like the simplest thing in the world. But it's not long before most friends, boys or girls, begin to feel at least a little bit of the strain that comes when two people care and depend on one another. A friend can be easily offended and hurt. A friend can become jealous. A friend can also disappoint you, and what you thought was an easy, happy relationship can sometimes turn sour.

While there are no tricks to keeping friends, there are certain sensitive areas that all friendships have in common. Being aware of these areas can't save a doomed friendship, but it may be able to help you stay friends with the people who really matter to you and improve the relationship you've got with them.

Being a good friend means not being a selfish friend. Do you show as much interest in her as she shows in you? Do you listen when she talks about problems, and do you respond with her needs in mind, not yours? Do you remember the special or important things happening in her life, and do you follow up on how they've gone?

Being a good friend means being able to be honest enough to enhance your relationship but not so honest that you hurt your friend's feelings. Are your criticisms of your friend constructive? Do you apologize when you realize you've done something hurtful to your friend? Do you admit to your faults without making too many excuses?

Being a good friend means being a sensitive friend. Are you aware of your friend's vulnerabilities, and are you careful to be sensitive to them? If you realize lately that your friend may be envious of certain things you've accomplished, are you watching out not to rub it in in her presence? When you notice your friend's in a bad mood, do you acknowledge it and try to cheer her up? When your friend needs your help, do you give that priority over other, maybe less important things?

Being a good friend means having realistic expectations in your friendship. Do you appreciate that your friend can not be exactly for you what you are for her? Do you recognize that she has her own needs and can't always be available to you when you feel you need her? Do you accept that there are certain things about you that even your best friend might not understand, if for no other reason than that she's not you?

Being a friend can mean helping your friend feel good about herself. Does she know what you like about her? Are you generous with your compliments, time, and possessions? Are you nice to her most of the time, and do you try to make up for it when you're not?

A point made earlier, in the dating section of this book, holds true here as well: caring enough to think about the other person's feelings, and to look at yourself objectively, can only make for stronger relationships.

What Do I Do If My Best Friend Betrays Me?

It can happen in the best of friendships. Someone who you've believed knows and understands you like no one else does, someone who you thought really liked you, does something that hurts you so much, you wonder if you'll ever be able to forgive her. Maybe she's talked to a classmate about something that was meant to remain your secret. Maybe she's made trouble for you and your boyfriend, or else taken a stand against you in public. Maybe she's ignored you at a time when you know she knew you needed her most.

There are occasions when little things a friend does can become very annoying. Usually it's just a matter of time before you cool off and don't feel bothered anymore. But with more serious incidents, you are likely to feel betrayed, and getting over it can be very difficult indeed.

Chances are you feel so hurt that it's all you can think about. Sometimes you can feel so angry that you don't know what to do with your rage. All you keep thinking is that she shouldn't have done that; you wouldn't have done that to her, and she knew how it would make you feel. How can you go on as friends now that this has happened?

It's probably a good idea if you are feeling that way to stop before you run to your friend to vent your rage. There will be plenty of time to tell her how angry and hurt you are. In the beginning, at least, you may want to give yourself time to think it through.

Since you feel so strongly, there's probably no doubt that you've been wrong, at least on some level. Still you should consider that maybe you are being a little too sensitive, or there was something that you did that precipitated your friend's unfriendly behavior. As certain as you may be of your friend's guilt, you may still want to think about what you might have done to contribute to the incident. It doesn't excuse a spiteful act, but realizing that you've been at another time maybe equally insensitive or mean may temper your feelings a bit.

If, after that, you still feel doubtful about the future of your friendship, you may want to seriously think about what it would be like not to be friends anymore. If you had a long or deep friendship, you probably would miss it. Think, if you can, about the qualities your friend has that you really like. Maybe she's given you better insights into your life than anyone else has, or maybe there's no one else you can have as much fun with. How would you feel about losing all of these things in this friend?

Then think about whether or not you could have been expecting too much from your friends. All friends cannot be all things. In fact, none can, including yourself. Unless you remember that, you're bound to be disappointed. Try and think about the incident as a clue to just one problem area in your friend's character, not as a case against her in total. In the future you may want to be careful not to depend on her in the particular way that she disappointed you. If, for example, she exposed a secret of yours, in the future you may want to be careful about what you confide in her. In the meantime, you may also want to look for or nurture another relationship in which you can trust that your secrets will be kept confidential. That's why it's good to have a few friends, each with their own strengths and weaknesses. Separately they may not be perfect, but together they could offer you all the things you've ever wanted from friendship.

What If My Parents Don't Like My Friends?

It happens to almost everyone. You bring home a friend and your mother or father either snubs her, stares at her, or acts in a way that you know means disapproval. Or maybe it's not until after your friend leaves that you find out. Your mother may ask you questions that suggest she's suspicious of your friend. Or you might know simply because she's not making the kind of remarks she usually does when she likes someone you bring home. Surely, the same could happen when you bring home a boy. In fact, with a boy it could be worse.

There are lots of reasons why parents may not like their children's friends. Many are good reasons; some may not be so valid. But the bottom line is that when parents react strongly, it usually means they are scared for their children. They're worried about how a person might threaten or influence you. It sometimes helps to understand, as unreasonable as you think it might be, that a parent's disapproval is different from a friend's. Parents may be more concerned for your well-being, more afraid for you, and, because of the intimate relationship they have with you, may be less able than a friend to separate their own fears, likes, and dislikes from yours.

It's not hard to figure out when parents don't like a friend. The hard part is knowing what to do about it.

To start with, you might want to find out their reasons. Some parents make it very obvious. They'll come right out and tell you how they feel about someone you know. They may even go so far as to tell you they don't think you should be friends with the person or that he or she isn't allowed in their house.

If it's not clear, however, ask. Is your friend unkempt, or does he or she appear to be under the influence of drugs? Your parents might be afraid that you will be tempted with something that isn't good for you. Has your friend gotten into trouble, or does he or she have a reputation in your town? It might worry your parents that, simply through association with this person, you too will get a reputation. In neither case are your parents necessarily right, but it's not hard to understand why they might worry.

If you want to keep the particular person as a friend, you might want to level with your mother and say something on the order of, "I know you don't like Jane because of some of the things you've heard about her. People say she takes a lot of drugs and all that. Well, it's true, she does do some drugs, but that's her business. She doesn't get me involved in it and it's not because of that that I like her." Tell your mother what you like about your friend. You might not be able to persuade her, but there's always a chance (especially if you don't lose your temper in the argument) that you will be able to change your parents' minds.

There's also the chance that your parents have the story all wrong, in which case you should set them straight on the facts in a calm, positive manner. Try and explain where you think the rumors got started and point out that everyone who really knows her is aware of the truth.

Maybe your parents don't like your friend because he or she is from a different background than yours. You might not think that's a good enough reason to dislike someone and you might be right, but your parents, because of what they were taught growing up, might feel very suspicious of anyone too different from themselves. If that's the case, there's a chance that nothing you say will convince them otherwise. It will compromise your friendship, for sure, but it doesn't have to destroy it.

Whatever you do, however, don't overreact to their seemingly unfair judgments. If you don't make a big deal about your parent's disapproval, they may slowly come around to your way of thinking. Your ability to understand where they may be "coming from" will speak louder for your ability to be your own person than any amount of yelling would.

Most importantly, when there is a disagreement between you and your parents, try to encourage

an open-minded discussion of the different issues involved. That's hard when it comes to
something as sensitive and emotional as friendships. But if you manage to do so, maybe your
parents could understand your side and maybe
you could understand theirs. And there's even a
chance that you'd find you don't disagree with
each other so much after all.

AT AND AROUND SCHOOL

School is clearly an important part of your life. By now you've had many years to get used to school routines, responsibilities, and pressures. Rules and regulations and course requirements are probably old hat to you. But what about your social life at school? It's not the reason you go to school, but it is an integral part of being there. And unlike academic codes, social codes can be undefined, contradictory, and just plain hard to understand.

Are Cliques A Good Or Bad Thing?

Cliques, gangs, or groups are an inevitable part of socializing, especially, it seems, in junior high and high school. You may not be part of any group in particular, but chances are you know exactly what the social divisions are within your school and what each group stands for. You may be more sympathetic to one group than you are to another, but finding yourself being drawn into one that you're a little less sure of.

If you've thought it out at all, you're probably also beginning to realize that being associated with a group has its advantages and disadvantages. It's true that a group automatically gives you a large circle of friends, but does it allow for the kind of privacy you may want every once in a while? Belonging to a group usually means there is always something to do and rarely the problem of having to decide on your own about what you want to do. Of course, going along with group consensus can also mean not having the time to figure out your own interests. Groups can get political and sometimes mean. What if the group you're finding yourself involved with doesn't accept your best friend? Or what if you're feeling that staying in a group might involve engaging in activities you're not sure you approve of?

Knowing how to act in these types of situations can be a little rough. Whether you're on the inside, or the outside thinking of getting in, you may want to take some of the following issues into consideration:

• What is the group's reputation? Are the members known for their good behavior, style or dress, or type of extracurricular activity? How do teachers refer to the group? What about parents? Do you think the reputation they have is a true one? In either case, do you want to become associated with whatever it is that is assumed of the group, right or wrong?

• Who is the group leader? Most groups have one, or if not that, a small group of people who seem to be just a bit more influential than others. Do you respect these people? Do you like them?

• How is being in the group affecting your schoolwork? Does it allow you enough time to do your homework? Are your grades as good now as they were before you were in the group?

• How is being in the group affecting your relationships with other people? Is it insulating you from other people, or is it allowing you to meet more?

• Do you feel like yourself in the group? Do people in it accept you as an individual, or are you expected to conform to a group norm?

• What role do you play in the group? Are you a leader or a follower, or someone who does a little bit of each depending on the situation? Are you happy with this position?

Groups and cliques are made up of individual people, and you probably will find yourself drawn to some of these individuals more than others. Take the time to develop these relationships. They'll offer you the opportunity to express yourself, feel more like an individual, and get to know another person a little more deeply than you would in the average group situation. You might just find that the other person is as happy as you are to establish a more personal kind of relationship.

If, after some thought, you decide that you either want to get out of the group you're in, or stay associated with it but not so exclusively, you could feel a lot of negative reactions from the clique. Taking time out for youself or other friends may seem hostile to members of the group. But try and remember you are not "wronging" them in any way. To want to feel free is not to be disloyal. After all, it's natural to want to separate yourself from the group every once in a while. They may be curious as to where you are; you can tell them if you want, but you don't necessarily have to consult with them before you go.

There are ways of staying part of a group without being saturated by it. You can spend a little time each afternoon with the group but not the whole afternoon as some other people do. Or else you can take a couple of days off to devote to your own interests. Over the phone you can find out what you missed, and stay informed that way.

How Can I Be In A Group, But Still Feel Like My Life Is All My Own?

Try sharing your interests and your outside friends with the group. If it's music lessons you take on the outside, play the instrument you're learning for some of your closer friends in the group. If it's a special hobby, for instance, macrame, you may want to teach a few members of the group how you do it. Everything you do is part of you. As long as you don't keep your interests and friends secret, after a while they should become an accepted aspect of who you are.

Why Does Competition Seem To Get Out Of Hand Sometimes?

Competition within bounds can be a very good thing. It can stimulate people to strive to do their best. But, like everything else, it's the degree to which people compete and the attitude which they bring to it that makes the difference between a good and bad experience.

Some people are very competitive with most things they do. Even in what seem to be unimportant areas, these people push to be the best often at any cost. In actuality, they often do very well in sports, in school, and in acquiring other skills. Very competitive people are usually very hard on themselves when they don't do as well as expected. And to highly competitive people, even very good is not good enough.

At the other extreme are the people who avoid competition altogether. If getting a part in a play means auditioning against fifteen other people, these people probably wouldn't try out at all, no matter how much they actually want the part. Chances are they would also favor solo sports over team sports; in that way they end up competing maybe even harder against themselves than they might have against another person.

Though you may fall somewhere in the middle, competition is probably as central an issue in your life as it is in the world in general. Competition takes place in all settings. It happens between members of families in their homes, and among people who work together. In school you probably are most aware of competition in sports and in the classroom. But if you think about it, you'll realize that competition comes up in social circles as well. Just as a student may want to get the best grade on a history final, so may another want to be the most popular student in the school or the boy with the most girlfriends. Competition is one way people have of asserting themselves and judging how they compare to other people in a group.

You might have a friend who, when you're with boys, seems to have to prove that they find her more attractive than they find you. Maybe she's particularly aggressive and flirtatious when you're around. Probably, in this area at least, she feels inferior to you and competing outright for boys is her way of trying to make herself feel better about something she actually feels bad about.

Competition of this kind often means people are insecure about their position in a group. It can also mean that actively competing has been the way they've been taught in their families to achieve something.

Sometimes teachers may encourage you to compete with each other for grades. As long as it doesn't get mean or too disappointing this kind of competition can be exciting and challenging. The trouble is, sometimes it's only the few winners who feel good about the competition after it all.

If you find yourself competing within a friendship, you're probably also finding that the relationship is becoming more tense and strained. You may want to honestly talk it over with your friend and try to find out why you're relating to each other that way. Probably there are qualities that each of you has that the other finds enviable. Reinforce each other's good points and try to remember that you can't measure each other by the same scale. You are different and special, each in your own right. With this understanding, you could be able to enjoy each other's company more.

The trick is to not make another person feel inferior, while you're busy trying to see yourself be successful. And the only way to do this is to remember other people's feelings. You can strive for great things without talking about it incessantly. And you can appreciate other people's successes without feeling that it chips away at your own.

I Get Very Nervous At Dances. Must I Always Feel That Way? How Can I Be More Relaxed At A Dance?

Most schools offer dances. If you haven't been to one already, you'll probably have the chance to go to one soon. Dances can make you feel awkward at first. It may feel strange to suddenly be thrown into a room with the same people you've been in class with all day. You may feel pressured to have fun, and as a result you suddenly may be a little shy and self-conscious. Maybe you don't think you know how to dance.

Luckily, these days, lots of forms of dancing are acceptable. You might feel like everyone's watching you, but if you're enjoying yourself and doing what feels comfortable to you, you won't stand out. And you probably won't worry about it, either. Dancing is meant to be fun. You might not want to spend all night dancing with someone you don't particularly like, but there's no reason not to dance with him a few times. And if there's someone you'd like to dance with who hasn't asked you yet, you don't need to necessarily wait for him to approach you. You can go up and talk to a boy you want to dance with and simply start dancing. You can ask him to join you and some other people in a group dance, or you can make a point of standing within his line of sight and hope that, noticing you, he'll ask you to dance.

A word of warning. Sometimes school dances get out of hand. You could be having so much fun that you might forget that you're at school and that there are teachers and administrators around to enforce school rules. Remember that the next day you will be back in the classroom again with the same people, and adjust your behavior accordingly.

Are There Things I Can Do To Improve My Social Life?

Because it's easier, most people in group situations get established with a few people and activities and then tend not to move away from them. You can see it in school cafeterias where a lot of students may sit at the same table with the same people year in and year out, or on school buses in which nobody ever changes their seat.

If you're comfortable with your friends and your social activities in and around school, there's no reason to move around except to get more exposure to different types of people and activities. However, if you feel bored by what you do, a change in your social scene could help.

The best way to get to know new people is to join them in an activity. It's a lot easier than sitting down and talking to someone you don't know, and a lot more fun, too. Joining a club or a team is a good way to make new friends. At first you might feel like the outsider, but as soon as you have a place in the chorus, a part in the play, or a position on the field, you will begin to feel like a contributor to the group and that you have something in common with its members.

If you prefer solo activities, they can also offer you the opportunity to meet new people. Going to one gym regularly to work out will give you a chance to meet and get to know other people who do the same. You will notice that like yourself, other people come on a specific schedule. Soon you should recognize each other, and before long you'll probably be starting up a conversation.

Teamwork also promotes friendship, whether collecting money for charity, cleaning the streets, or campaigning for a political candidate. You will have a common purpose with other people doing the same work. And the mutual satisfaction of providing a service, will bring you closer to your workmates.

Accept invitations to social gatherings and parties even if you don't know many people at them. The thought of walking into a party where you know very few people is frightening, but try and keep a few things in mind. Your host or hostess probably would not have invited you if he or she thought you would not have a good time. There are probably other people at the party who don't know many people either. Just as you are looking to meet new and interesting people, so are the other party goers! You never know who you'll meet at a party or how unexpectedly comfortable you might feel. It's worth doing, even if you are anxious about the scene you will initially face when the door is opened.

PARTYING AT HOME

Parties are fun, but they're also hard work. They take a lot of planning and preparation.

If you've never thrown a party before but are thinking of having one, you don't have to be afraid. There are a few basic guidelines you can follow that will make the whole idea of it a little less overwhelming.

Think it out, prepare well enough in advance, and maybe even go in on it with a friend. It may be a lot of work, but sometimes pulling a party together can be as much fun as the party itself.

How Can I Make My Party At Home A Success?

There are many things to keep in mind. Consider these issues in the order in which they are listed.

1.—Decide on a date. Take into consideration vacation schedules, religious holidays, academic pressures, and your parents' and neighbors' routines. Pick a time when the most people will be available and the fewest people will be disturbed. Check with your parents and make sure that the date is all right with them.

2.—Figure out how big a party you want to have. If you want to keep it small, you'll have to be discriminating about whom you choose to invite, and consider carefully which people would get along with each other. For a small party you should also expect that you'll have to devote more attention to your guests than you would at a larger party, where people tend to take care of themselves. If you want it to be large, how large? How many people can your house or the room you've reserved for the party accommodate? Take safety and comfort into consideration. Do you want it to be a stand-up party or a sit-down one? Do you have enough chairs for the number of people you're considering? If you're providing food, do you want to spend the amount of money it would take to have enough food for a large number of people? Calculate how much it would cost to provide two sodas per person. Add on to that the costs of whatever snacks you might want to have. Do you want to spend that much money? If your parents are paying, do they want to spend that much money? What are your financial limitations, and what are your physical limitations? Choose the number of people you're going to have accordingly.

3.—Make up a guest list. Do you want to have a co-ed party or just girls? If you're favoring co-ed, are you prepared to handle the kind of things that might go on at a party where there are boys? Will you be inviting all the boys associated with the girls you like, or just the boys you know well? Are there people you're thinking about who may have caused trouble at other parties you've attended? Are you ready to take the risk that they might cause trouble at yours, too?

4.—Send out invitations. Call or ask around, but don't be too public or loud about it. You don't want to hurt the feelings of people you're not inviting. Be clear about the time and nature of the party. If it's for dinner, say so. If your parents want it over by eleven, include that, too. Give people at least a week's notice so that they don't make other plans. You may not have to ask for a formal RSVP, but do indicate that your friends should tell you when they have an idea about whether or not they can make it. That way you'll be able to estimate how many people you'll have, how much extra room you may have for others, and how much food you'll need to buy.

5.—Plan out how you're going to arrange your house or the room for the party and what special needs you'll have to make adjustments for. Where will you set up the food? Where will you set up the music? Are there enough clear surfaces for people to put down cups and glasses? Do you want to put covers on the table tops so they don't get soiled? Do you want to clear away any articles in the room that are breakable? If you've got a rug, and you plan on having dancing, maybe you should pick up the rug. Where will everyone put their coats? If in a closet, do you have enough hangers? Which bathroom in the house will be the public bathroom? Do you want to provide guests with towels and soap? Is there adequate ventilation in the room you've picked, and good enough acoustics to absorb the music if you're planning on having it up loud?

6.—Make up two checklists. One should be for what you'll need to get, and the other should be for what you'll need to do in order to be ready for the party. If you're throwing the party with a friend, divvy up the responsibilities and decide when they'll get done. If you're mailing out invitations, allow at least three days for the mail, in addition to the week's notice you are giving guests. Check the house for serving plates, plastic cups or glasses, and napkins. If you need more, add them to your list.

7.—Buy whatever food and supplies you'll need at least a few days in advance of the party. That way you won't have to worry about waiting on a long line a few hours before your party is scheduled to begin. Save all receipts for your mother, you and, your friend if you're sharing expenses, or simply for your own personal reference or guide to how much your next party might cost you. Make any food that needs to be precooked or prepared as much in advance of the party as you can without any of it spoiling. Decide how you're going to present the food, and set aside the serving utensils and platters you will need.

8.—Decide what you're going to wear early enough before the party so that you have time to iron or do the necessary mending. Pick something special if you want. There are some outfits you might choose to wear at a party that you wouldn't necessarily wear outside. Remember that you'll need to be comfortable enough doing what is needed during the course of the party: serving food, clearing space, etc.

If you're borrowing music from friends, make

sure they clearly identify what belongs to them so that they'll be sure to get it back after the party's over. Warn your neighbors that you're having a party. If you want, you may even invite them. It's a nice gesture, even if you're sure they'd never come.

9.—If your party is scheduled to start at 8:00, try to be dressed and ready by 7:30. Guests may not start arriving until 8:30, but you'll probably need a little time to cool down beforehand anyway. Once the furniture is arranged to your liking and you're all dressed, you may want to review your checklists one last time to make sure you've left nothing out.

10.—Be at your door to greet guests around the time you expect them to arrive. No matter how casual the party is, you're still the hostess. It is your responsibility to show your guests in, tell them where to put their coats, etc. It is also your role to help them feel welcome. When most of your guests have arrived, you may join the party.

Circulate and see how everyone's doing. Check the food table. Are you running out of anything? Does it need to be straightened out? Pick up any stray cups or napkins. It will leave you less work in the end and contribute to a general sense of order at your party. Look around the room and get a sense for the party. Are your guests mingling, or are they sticking in the same spots with the same people? Is there one large group of people who are staying separate from the rest of the party? Do there appear to be people who are isolated, alone, and not having a good time? You may want to let the group be, or you might want to see if you can introduce someone new into their circle, and bring one of them over to another group.

It's nice to give attention to people who are alone or looking uncomfortable. Parties aren't the easiest things for many people. You can either approach these people yourself or go over with a friend. Good hostesses are often able to instigate conversations without actually having to stay involved themselves. If one group at your party is acting too cliquish and you think it may be intimidating the rest of your guests, bring a few friends over and join them; that way they'll be forced to take other people into consideration.

Music can also affect the tempo and mood of the crowd. A group that seems a little stiff, might loosen up with a record that's upbeat and fun. A group that may be getting a bit rowdy can sometimes be calmed down with a record of softer, quiet music. If slow music is alienating too many people at your party, if there are only a few couples dancing, you may want to switch to music with a faster beat. You can't control what happens at your party, but you may be able to influence it.

If anyone at your party is doing something that's either embarrassing the rest of the group, putting any of you in danger, or being outwardly hostile or destructive, it is your responsibility as the hostess to try to control the situation. If, let's say, one couple is necking right in the middle of the party, creating an awkward atmosphere, you may want to say something on the order of, "Do you want to go somewhere else? I think you're embarrassing some people." If somebody starts a fight, even if it hasn't gotten physical, approach them immediately and tell them to leave your house. If they want to come back when they've calmed down they can, but while fighting they're threatening the well-being of your guests, taking the risk of breaking things, and spoiling the mood of your party. If they won't go, get your parent. If somebody arrives at your party drunk or stoned, recognize that there's a good chance they may become disruptive. If you're afraid of the effects he or she may have on the rest of your party or don't particularly trust how he or she will behave, ask the person to leave. If you don't and they later pass out at your party, you'll have a much bigger problem on your hands.

How Do I Enforce The Rules Of My House Without Losing My Friends?

In general, if you notice people getting involved in activities that are otherwise prohibited in your household, as hard as it is, you probably should say something to them. You may not have made the rules in your house, and you may not even agree with many of them, but as the sponsor of the party it's your job to enforce them. Friends should understand that by disobeying the rules they're only getting you into trouble. Try not to feel self-conscious about taking this authority. Simply say your parents don't allow whatever it is. Don't worry about it reflecting on you. Of course if you completely agree with your parents on an issue, it would speak well for you to come right out and say *you're* having trouble with a particular guest's behavior. In all likelihood everyone will view you as a strong, clear-headed person. The only person who might not is the guest you're asking to leave. But then what will you think of his or her judgment anyway?

Try to relax and have a good time. While it's hard to feel the sort of freedom a guest has at your own party, it is possible to have fun. There's no reason you can't dance and talk and enjoy it like everyone else, as long as you stay alert for problems. When you think it's time for the party to break up, flash the lights a few times—it's a universally understood signal. Invite a good friend to stay on to help you clean up. As fun as party preparations can be, so can the time after the party. You can clean up at your leisure without the pressure of guests about to arrive. And while you're doing it, you can review everything that happened during the night.

ETIQUETTE

Probably the best argument for at least having a knowledge of manners is that they make you feel comfortable, or at least more comfortable than you would feel if you didn't know them. They also make other people feel comfortable, and that's important, too.

Imagine being selected to represent your class at a formal dinner the mayor's office is giving. You probably would feel nervous no matter how well you were prepared. But how would you feel if throughout the evening you found yourself in different situations you didn't know how to handle? What if you came in and didn't know what to do with your coat, then didn't know how to introduce yourself to the other guests? What if you didn't know what to call somebody or found yourself stuck talking with someone else and didn't know how to get away? What if at dinner you didn't know what to do with all the utensils in front of you or how to politely ask for seconds if you were feeling hungry? Would you ask for help, watch what other people were doing, or feel embarrassed? Making a mistake wouldn't mean the end of the world. But don't you think you could have more fun or at least feel more relaxed if you didn't have to worry about the right way to act in a situation like this?

Knowing manners frees you to enjoy yourself to your fullest.

Restaurants Make Me Uneasy. What Should I Know About Them?

Most towns have at least one restaurant and many have a few. They can range from the corner delicatessen or local luncheonette to the fancier gourmet ones. Maybe you haven't gone out much yet; going out is costly and often saved for special occasions. But as you get older and gain more reasons to celebrate, you could find yourself visiting restaurants more and more. You will see that there's quite a variety of places around offering different atmospheres, different dishes, and probably a wide range of prices, too. Familiarizing yourself with the particulars of the restaurant you've chosen can only help to make your special nights out that much more relaxing and enjoyable.

What's The Best Way To Choose A Restaurant?

When choosing a restaurant, you may want to either read up on a few in a guidebook or ask around among friends or family for their recommendations. If you've got a limited budget, ask about the price range. If you're looking for a particular kind of atmosphere, you can ask about that, too. You can even judge these things for yourself if, let's say, you happen to be passing by a restaurant that looks good but you know nothing about. All restaurants are required to post their menus outside. You can find them showing either on a window or door. Read it through and decide whether or not the restaurant offers the kind of food you want to eat, and at a price you can afford. You may want to take a peek through the windows to get a feel for the atmosphere or even step inside to take a better look. Tell the host that that's what you're doing, and most won't mind.

Some restaurants take reservations and some don't. If you aren't sure about whether or not a restaurant you've chosen requires them, call to find out. Generally, if a restaurant does take reservations, it means that it's so popular you probably wouldn't be able to get a table there without them. When placing reservations, specify the time you will be coming to dinner, your name, and how many people will be in your party.

How Do I Behave Once I Get There?

A lot of restaurants, especially the fancier ones, have a host or hostess who greets you when you enter, and a place to also check your coats. Umbrellas, packages, raincoats, and boots can all be checked, too. The coat check attendant will give you a numbered ticket, tag, or receipt, which you turn in when you're ready to leave. Most attendants expect a small tip in exchange for their services.

If you enter a restaurant in which there's a line and you have reservations, first find the host or hostess and tell him or her that you've arrived. A line usually means that there are no empty tables at the moment. As they begin to open up, you will be seated according to your place in line, the number of people in your party, and what time you had reserved. Most headwaiters or hosts don't mind being asked how long a wait to expect for a table. They can't tell you exactly, but they may be able to give you an approximation.

If you're faced with a line at a restaurant where you haven't made reservations, you can follow a similar routine. Give the host your name. He or she is probably keeping a running list of arrivals. When an appropriate table clears, your name will be called.

Hosts, hostesses, headwaiters, or maitre d's also escort you to your table or else direct a waiter or waitress to accompany you. If a restaurant is crowded or even just full, it's generally not considered a good idea to question your table assignment. If, on the other hand, there are a number of empty tables and there's one you would prefer, there's no reason not to ask for it. Just be polite and say something on the order of, "Is it all right if we sit there instead?"

Follow the host to your table. He or she will probably expect the woman to come first. Once at the table he may wait for you to choose your seat and then help you with the chair. When a host does that, it could be awkward if you hesitate for too long in deciding where to sit or if you were to reach over him and pull out the chair yourself. The gracious way is to step aside, take your seat, then wait for the host to help maneuver it closer to the table. If you're not used to being helped with your chair, the whole ritual could feel kind of funny. If you don't know to expect it, however, it could feel even funnier.

Is There Any Special Way To Order?

Shortly after you've been seated, the waiter assigned to you will come to your table with menus and sometimes bread, rolls, and water. At some restaurants they offer what they call "house specials" or "specials of the house." A special is a dish cooked especially for that night that usually isn't listed on the menu. The waiter or waitress may describe the special, but generally he or she won't tell you the price. Some people might be embarrassed to ask but if money is an issue, or you're just curious, there's no reason why you can't.

Study the menu. After a waiter or waitress has seated you, he or she will usually leave you a good five to ten minutes before he/she comes back for your order. Consider the descriptions and the price of each dish. If you're being taken out either by adult friends or a date, avoid ordering the most expensive dishes. Look for something in the middle range that you might enjoy. If the waiter comes back to your table and you haven't decided yet, rather than make him wait, tell him you need a few minutes more to make up your mind. If nothing looks familiar to you, you may want to ask your waiter for an additional description of a particular dish, or you may want to make your decision based on category. Most menus are organized in such a way that all the spaghetti dishes, for example, are listed together, all the salad, roasts, fish, etc. If you like chicken, you probably can count on liking many of the chicken dishes on any given menu. Once you order, try not to change your mind. If the waiter or waitress is still at your table and you're sure you've made the wrong decision, you can ask politely if it's all right to switch. Otherwise, accept your choice. Once a waiter has placed an order in the kitchen, it's usually too late to change it.

In the interim, don't eat all the bread or crackers. It could spoil your appetite and make you look a little piggish.

Are My Table Manners Going To Embarrass Me?

Good table manners shouldn't be reserved for restaurants, but it's probably in restaurants that you'll be most happy that you know them.

The first table manner you'll want to observe after sitting down at your table is to place your napkin on your lap. Napkins serve a practical purpose. (You'll be happy you have one on your lap if you should accidentally drop any food.) But the point of placing one on your lap as soon as you sit down is also part ceremony. It is a way of marking the official beginning of a meal. Your napkin should stay in your lap throughout your meal except when you're using it. If for any reason you have to excuse yourself from the table, lay your napkin to the left of your plate, slightly folded over, and push your chair back in close to the table.

You should keep your hands in your lap and your arms off the table even if your food hasn't arrived yet. There's usually not that much room on the table for them anyway.

When your food arrives, don't rush to start, no matter how hungry you are. Check first to see that everyone else has been served and that you have all the things that you might need to eat comfortably.

If there's anything on the table you need that is not within your immediate reach, ask for it to be passed to you. Besides being considered bad manners, leaning across the table for a salt shaker can have disastrous effects.

Eat slowly. Cut your food in small enough portions so that you will be able to chew quietly and easily with your mouth closed. Cut your meat into pieces as you eat it, not all at once before you start. When you're finished with your knife, place it diagonally across the right-hand corner of your plate. Don't mix food together on your plate or fuss with it in any other way.

How Do I Eat Hard-To-Handle Food?

Hamburgers. A hamburger can be messy and embarrassing to eat, especially if it's big and juicy and has a number of condiments added on to it. It helps sometimes to cut the hamburger in half and eat it like a sandwich. You don't have to actually lean into your plate, but take care when you bite into your hamburger to make sure your plate is underneath it to catch any possible drippings.

Baked Potatoes. In restaurants, baked potatoes often come wrapped in tin foil and slit down the middle. You can squeeze the potato open slightly with your fingers, but if you want to season it with sour cream or spices, do that with a fork. Use your fork also to scoop the potato out one portion at a time. Leave the skin in the foil.

Corn on the Cob. You may be used to eating corn on the cob in one fell swoop at picnics, but in more formal situations it's considered better manners to eat it one bite at a time.

Fish. Fish that hasn't been boned can be very difficult to eat. If you're ordering whole fresh fish, you may want to request that they bone it in the kitchen. (Many restaurants do anyway.) Otherwise, slit the fish from head to tail with your knife. Open the fish out flat, using your knife and fork, and insert the tip of your knife under the backbone. Gently remove as much of the skeleton as you can and place it on the side of your plate. If you find small bones as you eat, discreetly remove them from your mouth by hand and leave them on your plate.

Lobster. Break off the small claws first. You can either suck or chew the meat out of them. Next break open the larger claws, (usually a shell cracker will be provided), and remove the meat from the insides with your fish fork. Pick the meat from the body of the lobster with your fork and carefully dip small pieces into the butter, one at a time. Eating lobsters can be messy no matter how hard you try to be neat. That's why restaurants will frequently give you bibs to use while you're eating.

Chicken. In restaurants, chicken should be eaten with a fork and a knife. Bones should be left altogether in one corner of your plate.

Spaghetti. Spaghetti should be eaten twisted around your fork, not slurped. Twirl a few strands at a time, either by resting your fork against your plate or up against the inside of a spoon. The smaller a portion you take, the less of a chance that the spaghetti will unravel.

Are There Any Rules On Tipping?

Tipping is expected at pratically all restaurants. A standard tip is between 15 and 20 percent of your total bill. If you are especially pleased with the service you received, you may want to leave more than the standard amount. You may also want to thank the waiter as you leave.

Do I Really Need To Watch My Manners At Home?

Unless you live in a formal household, you probably don't observe the same rules of etiquette at home as you might outside. Still, manners apply at home as much as they do in other places; they're just different.

Maybe you don't call your father sir or stand up every time your mother enters the living room, but that doesn't mean you shouldn't acknowledge a parent's arrival when he or she comes home from work or help your mother or father carry packages from the car after they've been grocery shopping.

Manners at home are mostly a matter of being considerate. If your mother or father makes lunch for you every day, maybe it's not necessary to thank them each morning. But if your father puts in a special treat for you, it would be rude to not at least say, "Thank you" or acknowledge that you appreciated the "extra something." Similarly, if you need help from one of your parents with homework or chores, or if you just need a favor, it's nice to first say, "Please." It's a simple rule, one you might have been taught a long time ago. Maybe you're only now beginning to understand the purpose of it. You know that most parents are more than happy to help out their children, but parents are people, too. They get tired like you do, their feelings get hurt, and, like you, they may also feel at times like they're not appreciated enough. "Please" and "Thank you" may be small things, but sometimes they can go a long way.

If you were in a restaurant at a table with a few people and you had to get up and go, for whatever reason, you probably wouldn't leave without excusing yourself first. It's a good idea at home, too. Some parents like their children to ask to be excused from the dinner table. Others like their children to at least say they're leaving. Maybe your parents haven't expected you to do either. Still, getting up and walking away without any explanation is disconcerting. It says you don't particularly care about the other people at the table. Even a parent can be offended by that.

Being sloppy in common rooms around the house is different than being sloppy in your own room. It's bad manners; it imposes on other people and requires that someone clean up after you. If you get up from the kitchen table and forget to push your chair in, someone else probably eventually will. If you leave your books strewn around the living room rug and your parents are having company, someone will probably gather up your books before the company arrives. Maybe you're used to having someone pick up after you, or maybe you think that's what parents are for. If that's the case, think about what it might feel like to be your own mother or father. Think about coming home tired after school only to cook dinner, or fixing up your bedroom for a special friend just to have someone mess it up again. Altogether your job wouldn't be a very easy one. Neither is your parents'. That's one reason why manners help. They show the other person that you appreciate their efforts. And that can make any job easier.

And finally, if you school yourself to remember your manners at home, they will probably come more automatically when you are socializing outside. If they become second nature, you won't have to give them so much concious thought when you really should just be enjoying yourself.

How Should I Act At Formal Affairs?

Maybe you've never been invited to a fancy party. Some day you might. Whether you go alone, with a friend, or with someone in your family, there are certain proper manners you will want to observe.

If you're not greeted at the door by your host or hostess, ask someone when you enter where you should leave your coat. Even if you're planning on staying only a short while, it's better to leave your coat in the allotted place rather than carry it around with you. Otherwise it looks like you're in a rush to leave. Look around the room for the person who invited you to the party or function. Even the most formal parties are thrown by someone, and it's polite when you arrive to greet the person and in some fashion or another thank him or her for having you.

If you're introducing yourself to people you don't know, shake hands. Even with those you do know it's nice to do. Don't necessarily wait for the other person to offer his or her hand. Also, shake the other person's hand firmly. A weak handshake can be embarrassing and says to another person that you're not too enthusiastic about meeting him or her.

If you like to excuse yourself from a conversation, politely wait for an opportune time. Try not to interrupt someone in mid-sentence, before he or she has finished making a point, or in the middle of a joke or a story. (This also applies for all situations. Interrupting is bad manners no matter where you do it.) Wait for a pause in the conversation and say something on the order of, "It was nice talking to you," or "I really should find so and so." If you've met someone for the first time, it's polite to also say, "It was nice meeting you."

Call adults Mr., Miss, or Mrs., unless they invite you to call them by their first names.

If hors d'oeuvres are being served, take one at a time. You don't want to spoil your appetite or not leave enough for the other guests.

Avoid staying in one corner or with one person for too long a period of time. It's good to circulate, for the sake of your own exposure to different people as well as being a help to making the function a successful social occasion. As a guest you should think of yourself as a participant, not just someone out for your own good time.

If it's a sit-down meal you're attending, wait for the host or hostess to seat you. At most formal functions seating is arranged beforehand. If there are place cards, look around the table for yours and sit down where you find it.

It's nice to say hello to the people on either side of you even if you don't know them.

Put your napkin on your lap and try to keep your arms off the table. Don't start eating anything, even bread, until everyone is seated.

Using the right utensils at formal dinners can

be a little complicated only because there are often more of them than you're used to. Generally, utensils are set around a plate in the order they should be used, starting the farthest out from the plate, and ending with the last utensil to be used nearest it. Your salad fork will probably be on the outside of your dinner fork and your fruit salad spoon probably on the outside of your soup spoon. If that's not the case you can judge by the way the utensils look. Your largest fork is always your dinner fork, your largest knife your meal knife, and your largest spoon your soup spoon. Small forks are for salads or cake and small spoons are for desserts or coffee. Sometimes places are set with fish or butter knives. A fish knife is generally flatter and wider than the usual knife and often placed horizontally right above your plate. A butter knife is usually a miniature of a regular knife. If too many utensils confuse you, stop and watch what other people are using.

When you leave a formal party (or any party, for that matter), it's always good practice to say good-bye to your host or hostess first. Thank them for having you, and if you like, tell them why or how you enjoyed yourself.

Write a thank you note, either when you get home or within a few days after the event. You don't have to say much in a thank you note in order for it to be appreciated. You may want to comment on the food or mention the names of people you particularly enjoyed speaking with. Just saying thanks and that you had a good time is really enough. It shows that the host's or hostess's efforts have been appreciated.

CONCLUSION

Some feelings are hard to put into categories. They're vague and difficult to express, and therefore often the kinds of feelings that people tend to keep to themselves. You didn't have to read this book to find out that being a teenager isn't always as much fun as it's cracked up to be. If you're like most people your age, you've already had your share of embarrassing or awkward experiences at home, in school, and out and around town.

But what about those feelings that aren't as obvious or easy to understand? What chapter would you turn to in this book if you were feeling just plain sad or else so discouraged that you thought nothing would ever go right for you? These kinds of feelings have more to do with deep emotions and attitudes than any specific situations you might be in. They affect the way you feel in general and how you might react to normal disappointments. If you don't get a part ina school play, you could believe that you have no talent and that you should never try out for a play again. If a boy you like doesn't like you, you could think that no boy ever will.

The fact is that few things are as absolute as they seem when you're upset. Luckily, in life there are many chances and opportunities to improve on a bad experience. In other words, one bad date doesn't mean you're a failure with boys. You'll have many other chances.

And with a positive attitude, you will see that you have at least a little control over how things turn out in your life. With a bit of luck, your next date might just turn out to be the best one you've ever had.

And if luck isn't on your side, what then? You have yourself. Despite all of the good and bad things life might send your way, it's important to remember you, in your own unique way, can help to influence the consequences.

BIBLIOGRAPHY AND SUGGESTED READING

Baker, Eugene. **Your Manners Are Showing: A Handbook About Etiquette.** Elgin, Illinois: Child's World, 1980.

Burkhart, Katheryn Watterson. **Growing Into Love.** New York: G. P. Putnam's Sons, 1981.

Calderone, MD, Mary S. and Johnson, Eric W. **The Family Book About Sexuality.** New York: Harper and Row, 1981.

Comfort, Alex and Jane. **The Facts of Love.** New York: Ballantine, 1979.

Corsaro, Maria and Korzeniowsky, Carole. **STD: A Commonsense Guide.** New York: St. Martin's Press, 1980.

Gardner, Dr. James. **The Turbulent Teens.** San Diego: Oak Tree Publications, Inc., 1982.

Ginolt, Dr. Haim G. **Between Parent and Teenager.** New York: Avon, 1969.

Hoving, Walter. **Tiffany's Table Manners for Teenagers.** New York: Ives Washburn, Inc., 1961.

Johnson, Eric W. **Love and Sex in Plain Language.** New York: Bantam Books, 1977.

Kelly, Gary, ed. **Learning About Sex: The Contemporary Guide For Young Adults.** New York: Barron's Educational Series, Inc., 1977.

Landau, Elaine. **Teen Guide to Dating.** New York: Julian Messner, 1980.

Peck, Ellen. **How To Get a Teenage Boy and What To Do With Him Once You Get Him.** New York: Avon, 1974.

INDEX

The JUST FOR TEENS series

THE BEAUTY BOOK by Rubie Saunders

A one-volume practical guide to help you maximize your beauty potential!

THE DATING BOOK by Julie Cahn

A straightforward guide to relationships-how to make them work and grow.